Caroline Bingham was born in Hampstead in 1938, and educated at Cheltenham Ladies' College and Bristol University.

She has written numerous books mostly on Scottish subjects, which include *The Making of a King: the Early Years of James VI and I*; *James V, King of Scots*; *The Stewart Kingdom of Scotland, 1371-1603*; *The Kings and Queens of Scotland* and a two-volume biography of the Scottish king who became King of Great Britain, *James VI of Scotland* and *James I of England*.

CAROLINE BINGHAM

Land of the Scots
A Short History

Fontana Paperbacks

First published by Fontana Paperbacks 1983

Set in 11 on $12^{1}/_{2}$pt Linotron Garamond
Made and printed in Great Britain
by William Collins Sons & Co. Ltd, Glasgow

Contents

Author's Note

Land of the Scots was commissioned with a particular readership in mind. It is addressed to readers who have little or no previous acquaintance with Scottish history. Most of those readers will know something of the Scottish figures who have achieved international fame (of whom Mary, Queen of Scots is only one example) but they may welcome an opportunity to know more of the *dramatis personae* of Scotland's history. Other readers may be visitors to Scotland, who will immediately recognize that although Scotland is part of the United Kingdom (and has been so since the Union of Parliaments of 1707) its separate history, traditions, laws, culture and religion have given Scotland a national character very different from that of England. *Land of the Scots* is an attempt to tell in brief the story of Scotland, and at the same time to suggest how it has come about that Scotland retains its distinctive character, and may also possess the will to pursue its own political destiny again in the future.

The greatest satisfaction I could achieve through writing this book would be to arouse in its readers a wish to know more of the subject. In the hope that I shall have proved successful in so doing, I have provided a list of books for further reading which includes general histories, biographies, and books on particular topics to which the brevity of the text has necessarily allowed little space. I wish to acknowledge that the latest statistics on population, population movement, and the increase in the numbers of Gaelic speakers are derived from *Scotland, the Different* by Richard Bourne (*New Society*, 18 March 1982).

A small point which readers will notice is that the surname of the Royal House of Stewart becomes Stuart with the accession of Mary, Queen of Scots. Mary herself adopted the French spelling of her surname, and retained it on her marriage to her cousin Henry Stuart, Lord Darnley, whose father Matthew Stuart, fourth Earl of Lennox, had adopted it when he took French nationality in 1537.

For permission to reproduce photographs, the author is grateful to the following: British Library (St Margaret, David II with Edward III, and Charles I); University of Glasgow (James III and James V); Giraudon (James IV); Glasgow Art Gallery and Museum (Mary, Queen of Scots); National Portrait Gallery (James I, James VII and II, James Edward Stuart and Charles Edward Stuart) and National Galleries of Scotland (Charles II, Marquess of Montrose, Viscount Dundee, David Hume, Robert Burns, Thomas Chalmers, James Keir Hardie and Hugh McDiarmid).

Topographical Map of Scotland
(with Place Names and Modern Regions)

SHETLAND

ORKNEY
Kirk Wall

Cape Wrath
Pentland Firth
John O'Groats

WESTERN ISLES

NORTH UIST

SOUTH UIST

ERISKAY

RHUM

SKYE

SLEAT

Glenshiel

The Great Glen

HIGHLAND

Moray Firth

Elgin
Inverness
Peterhead

GRAMPIAN

Aberdeen

Fort Augustus

Braemar

Glenfinnan
Loch Shiel
Fort William
TAYSIDE
Brechin
Montrose

ARDNAMURCHAN
COLL

Glencoe

Dunkeld
Arbroath

MORVERN

STRATH

Crieff
Scone
Dundee

TIREE

MULL

Oban

CENTRAL
Perth
Falkland
St Andrews

ISLE OF IONA

Inveraray

Dunblane
Loch Leven
FIFE

Stirling
Dunfermline

Firth of Forth

LOTHIAN

Cambuskenneth

Dunbar

Dumbarton
Linlithgow

CLYDE

Renfrew
Edinburgh
Holyrood

BUTE

Glasgow
Newbattle
Lander
Berwick

Rothesay

KINTYRE

ARRAN

BORDERS
Birgham

Melrose
Kelso

Dryburgh
Roxburgh

Ayr

Jedburgh

DUMFRIES AND
GALLOWAY

Lochmaben

Dumfries

Dundrennan

Whithorn
Solway Firth

Battles in the History of Scotland
(with Old Provinces and Districts)

CAITHNESS

SUTHERLAND

Carbisdale 1650

ROSS

BUCHAN

Auldearn
1645

Culloden 1746

MORAY   MAR   Alford
1645

BADENOCH

ATHOL   ANGUS

Killiecrankie 1689

GOWRIE   Nechtansmere

Dunkeld 1045   685

Dupplin Moor
1332

MENTEITH   Sherriffmuir   FIFE

1715

Sauchieburn   Bannockburn   LOTHIAN

1488   1314

Falkirk   Prestonpans

Langside   1298 and 1746   Pinkie   1745   Dunbar 1296

1568   1547   and 1650

Largs   Carberry   Halidon Hill

1263   Bothwell   Stirling   Rullion   Hill 1567   1333

Bridge 1679   Bridge   Green

1297   1666   Carham-on-

Drumclog   Tweed 1018   Flodden 1513

Loudoun   1679

Hill 1307   Philiphaugh 1645   Homildon

LENNOX   1402

CARRICK   Arkinholme

1455   Neville's Cross

1346

GALLOWAY   Solway Moss

1542

'Battle of the Standard'
(Northallerton) 1138

CHAPTER ONE

The Making of Scotland
Prehistoric times to 1034

The long winter of the Ice Age relaxed its grip on northern Europe in about 6000 BC, and the unimaginable force of water released by the great thaw severed the British Isles from the Continent.

The British imagination is haunted by the idea of being marooned on a desert island with nothing except ingenuity and natural resources. Perhaps this is not a fantasy of urban man, sickened by alienation from the rhythms of nature; perhaps it is the oldest of racial memories, the purest atavism. For at the end of the Ice Age small groups of nomadic hunters were marooned on the newly formed British Isles to begin the long task of subjugating nature to the purposes of man.

How they began to do so can only be conjectured. Prehistoric sites are like the pieces of an unassembled jigsaw puzzle; every piece has an intriguing vignette on it, but the picture is fragmented. The earliest traces of human habitation in the north of Britain probably belong to little later than 6000 BC. At Morton, in Fife, traces of people who lived by hunting and fishing have been found. They, and their nearest known contemporaries, killed to eat, and moved on when they had exhausted such resources of the area as lay within their scope. On the coasts they ate stranded whales and caught seals and inshore fish. Inland, they followed herds of red deer and reindeer. Where they penetrated

11

the dark primeval forests they appear to have burned clearings to secure their camps against predators, which included bears and wolves.

In about 4000 BC the population was augmented by the coming of seaborne peoples, originating probably in the lands around the Mediterranean. They brought seedcorn and domesticated animals, and introduced the practice of agriculture. The establishment of territorial claims, which agriculture necessitated, probably led to a great deal more fighting than had ever taken place before. Perhaps the shocking fact that large groups of human beings began to fight each other gave rise to the myth of a non-violent golden age, however un-golden the life of early man may have been in other respects.

Permanent settlements, once established, left clearer evidence for archaeological research. One of the most vivid evocations of prehistoric life for the visitor to Scotland is to be found in Orkney, in the village of Skara Brae. Here, since no timber was available, the people built their houses and constructed their furniture of stone. Their now roofless cottages contain stone bed-boxes – which no doubt would have been filled with bedding of hides and dried vegetation – stone dressers, fireplaces and stools, and watertight stone floor-boxes, for keeping shellfish. The proximity of the rubbish heaps to the houses has suggested that the people lay in bed to eat their meat and shellfish and threw the bones and shells outside. The realization that people have always striven to improvise comfort, even in the most inhospitable surroundings, makes this remote past seem movingly familiar.

The people of Skara Brae, who lived longer before Christ than we live after Him, sought comfort and feared disaster just as people do now. In approximately 2500 BC the whole community fled from a violent storm. What became of the people no one knows, but their village, mercifully free from human remains, was overwhelmed by drifts of sand, to lie undisturbed by later depredations or developments, for twentieth-century men to discover and wonder at.

The increasing necessity for defence makes later prehistoric buildings less attractive. 'Crannogs', or lake villages built on stilts, must have been intolerably damp, and frequently fog-bound or flooded; while 'souterrains', or earth houses, were no more than gloomy human burrows. 'Brochs', the stone towers shaped like the cooling towers of power stations, built by tribal chiefs to afford defence and shelter for their followers, must have been unbearably overcrowded in times of strife; but they were so well built that they were still occupied by squatters during the Middle Ages, and substantial remains of them survive to this day. The most intact example is the Broch of Mousa, in Shetland.

Hunters, agriculturalists and warriors successively swelled the population of North Britain, and each society introduced its own skills and left its characteristic remains. The prehistoric peoples buried their illustrious dead under grave-mounds of various designs, and placed beside them grave-goods which suggest that they imagined an afterlife which would not be very different from life in this world. The jade-headed axes found on earlier sites, and the elaborate gold jewellery of the later Celtic chiefs, suggest that for long ages North Britain had been linked with a widely disseminated prehistoric civilization of which all the clues have not yet been either found or deciphered.

Prehistory and history meet when the tribal society of North Britain encountered the highly organized power of the Roman Empire. Julius Caesar's invasions of southern Britain in 55 and 54 BC were scarcely more than reconnaissance expeditions. The Roman Conquest began in earnest in the reign of the Emperor Claudius, who gained power in AD 41. By 78 the Roman province of Britannia included most of what later became England, and parts of Wales. In that year the Roman governor, Gnaeus Julius Agricola, turned his attention to the unconquered north, which the Romans called Caledonia.

It was fortunate both for posterity and for Agricola himself that the historian Tacitus was his son-in-law, for Tacitus' account of Agricola's campaign is the first literary text to provide information about North Britain. Agricola ascertained that the mainland of Britain was an island, and resolved to make the northern coastline the frontier of the province. In AD 83 he marched north with three legions and established a strong base at Inchtuthil, in Perthshire, as well as a system of defence in depth behind

The Roman invasion provoked the resistance of a great tribal confederation under a leader called Calgacus, whose name means simply 'the swordsman', but such a name doubtless implies that he was a warrior hero. He had sufficient prestige to command an army of 30,000 men. This great force, headed by a warrior aristocracy which went to war in chariots like Homeric heroes, commanded by a man who probably thought and fought like Achilles, stood little chance against the discipline of the legions. Calgacus was defeated in 84 at the Battle of Mons Graupius, a site which has not been identified with certainty, though it is thought to have been on the Perthshire edge of the Grampians.

The next year Agricola was recalled to Rome. Perhaps his tour of duty was ended in accordance with routine; or perhaps, as was believed at the time, his success had aroused the jealousy of the Emperor Domitian. *Britannia perdomita et statim amissa* – 'Britain completely conquered and at once thrown away' – was Tacitus' bitter comment.

Historical experience was to prove that often North Britain would appear to have been conquered completely, but always the impenetrable terrain would aid its defenders. A victory on the fringe of the Highlands, like Mons Graupius, could assure at most the conquest of the Lowlands. The division between Highlands and Lowlands is not an east-west cartographical parallel, but a wavering diagonal which bisects Scotland from north-east to south-west, so that almost the whole of the eastern seaboard is Lowland. In the Highlands lie the great mountain massifs and the long sea lochs, creating an area in which conquest, administration and even ordinary communications were at first impossible and long remained difficult.

The Romans never attempted to penetrate the Highlands. After the recall of Agricola, later Roman rulers settled for an artificial east-west frontier, far south of Agricola's original ambition of the natural boundary of the northern coast. In 122 the Emperor Hadrian visited Britannia and ordered the building of a great wall from the Tyne to the Solway. For many centuries Hadrian's Wall looked like a monument to a long-dead system of imperialism; but in the present century the construction of the Berlin Wall suggests how awe-inspiring and effective a barrier the Roman Wall must have been in the heyday of the Empire.

Hadrian's Wall was not, however, an immutable frontier. Twenty years later, the governor Lollius Urbicus attempted to move the frontier further north, and built the Antonine Wall from the Forth to the Clyde. The last Roman offensive took place in 208, when the old Emperor Septimius Severus advanced as far as the Moray Firth and, stricken with mortal sickness, had himself carried south in a litter to die, at Eboracum, the Roman York.

Thereafter, the Romans accepted the invincibility of the northern tribes. Hadrian's Wall was fixed as the frontier of the province and the Empire, though a few military outposts were maintained to the north of it. Caledonia remained unconquered, though not wholly unaffected by Rome. Cultural infiltration from the Empire took place through trade, intermarriage and religious influence. The later Romans knew the names of seventeen northern tribes, though they only encountered members of those in proximity to the Wall and its outposts. Consequently they were inclined to refer to all the dwellers beyond it, with vague generalization, as 'Caledonii' or 'Picti'. The tenuous connection between Rome and Caledonia was severed during the early years of the fifth century AD, when the legions were withdrawn from Britannia to deal with the threat to Rome itself of the Barbarian invasions from Eastern Europe and beyond.

The inhabitants of the abandoned Roman province were left to defend themselves against the attacks of seaborne Teutonic invaders. The medieval romances of King Arthur take up the long-remembered echoes of the Romano-Britons' struggle for a lost cause. The real

Arthur was probably a tribal chief, a latter-day Calgacus, and not the king of all Britain, for in the fifth century there was no unifying influence which could have produced such a man. Nonetheless, it remains to be explained why some of the Arthurian legends are connected with the Scottish Border country, and others with Cornwall. Perhaps he fought, and lived for a time, wherever he could inspire the spirit of resistance. The haunting figure of King Arthur remains one of the mysteries of the 'dark ages'.

A long night of strife closed the story of Roman Britain, and when the first light of the Middle Ages began to grow, it revealed a changed world. The invaders who overwhelmed Roman Britain established the seven kingdoms of Anglo-Saxon England. In the north four kingdoms emerged which contributed to the making of Scotland.

The largest of these four kingdoms was that of the Picts, which extended lengthwise from Orkney to the Forth. The Picts are as mysterious in their origins as in their later disappearance. They are believed to have been Celts, or at least part-Celtic, but their lack of literature makes conjecture hazardous. Their overwhelmingly consonantal inscriptions, incised in stone, have so far defied translation. Perhaps some scholar of the future will decipher:

BESMEQQNANAMMOVVEZ

or

ETOCUHETIS AHEHHITANAN HCCVVEVV NEHHTONS

The elusiveness of the Picts is all the more disturbing because they left these tantalizing clues.

In their sculpture they left more attractive evidence of their skills. With exquisite delicacy they carved their so-called 'symbol-stones', of which the earlier were incised slabs and the later low reliefs. Pre-Christian stones were incised with animal and abstract designs, and Christian reliefs with interlace-patterned crosses, animals, figures, hunting scenes and possibly classical themes. Were some of the early designs those which the Picts, by painting or tattooing, depicted on themselves, thus acquiring the name which the Romans gave them?

To the south of the Picts, in the land which is now Lothian, lived the Angles, who pushed northward from the Anglo-Saxon Kingdom of Northumbria. When the Northumbrian power was its zenith, its King Egfrith aspired to conquer the Picts. He marched north to meet defeat at the hands of the Pictish King Brudei, at the Battle of Nechtansmere, near Dunnichen in Forfarshire, in 635. Some scholars believe that this battle was decisive in preserving the embryonic Scotland from an Anglo-Saxon conquest.

In the south-west of present-day Scotland lay the Kingdom of Strathclyde, which incorporated part of the present Cumbria. It was the most long-lived of the ancient British kingdoms, formed by the peoples who had been cornered by the advance of Rome. Its inhabitants were Welsh-speaking Britons.

The Scots, who were to give their name, their culture and their traditions to the later Kingdom of Scotland, occupied Argyll and its adjacent islands, which they called Dal Riata. They had colonized the area from a parent kingdom of the same name, in Northern

Ireland, roughly coterminous with County Antrim. It is one of the oddities of history, and therefore easily remembered, that Ireland was called 'Scotia' before it was called Ireland, and that the Scots came from Ireland and colonized Scotland. In about 500 the colony of Dal Riata became a kingdom when Fergus Mor mac Erc (i.e., Fergus the Great, son of Erc) who was a member of the royal family of Irish Dal Riata made himself King of Scots on the mainland.

From Fergus Mor mac Erc all the ensuing Scottish dynasties could claim descent. The link with the royalty of Irish Dal Riata grew tenuous, but it remained unbroken, for when the succession failed in the male line an heir in the female line survived to inherit. The blood of Fergus flowed through the old Scottish royal houses of Alpin and Dunkeld, to those of Bruce and Stewart, and at last through Elizabeth, daughter of King James VI of Scotland and I of England, it was transmitted to the House of Hanover, so that it continues in the present Royal Family of Great Britain.

In the later Middle Ages a mythical pedigree was invented for Fergus, which traced his descent from one Fergus, son of Ferehard, who was supposed to have flourished in about 330 BC; but when later scepticism caused this genealogical graft to wither, the genuine descent of the Scottish kings from Fergus Mor mac Erc conferred a sufficiently prestigious antiquity.

Just over sixty years after the founding of the Scottish Kingdom of Dal Riata, St Columba, who was an Irish prince, crossed from the parent kingdom. In 563 he established his monastery on the Island of Iona. His arrival was not missionary in the first instance, for the Scots of Dal Riata were already Christian, and had probably come from Ireland as converts of St Patrick. Indeed, a later legend claimed that St Patrick had prophesied the kingly destiny of Fergus and his descendants.

Columba, besides being a man of outstanding sanctity, was also an astute politician. His influence, both religious and political, strengthened Dal Riata in its relations with the greater power of the neighbouring Picts. St Columba advanced the conversion of the Picts, though his work was continued and completed by others.

The Scots of Dal Riata and their great saint were not the first Christians to reach North Britain. Christianity may have been the legacy of the Roman legions, for Tertullian wrote in 208 *Britannorum inaccessa Romanis loca Christo vero subdita*: 'Among the Britons places unreached by the Romans have come under the rule of Christ.' Dwellers beyond the Wall who met Roman converts may well have carried Christian belief to the regions to which Tertullian vaguely referred.

St Ninian, who built his church of white stone, the *Candida Casa*, beside Wigtown Bay, before the end of the fourth century, is the first Christian missionary who is known by name. According to Bede, Ninian was a Briton who had been instructed in Rome, and consecrated a bishop. Legends attributed to him an incredible mileage of missionary journeys; but probably many of those undertaken by his followers came to be ascribed to the Saint himself. By the end of the seventh century the labours of the great missionary saints, Ninian, Columba, Kentigern, Moluag, Maelrubha, and of a host of forgotten auxiliaries, had spread Christianity throughout the four kingdoms of North Britain. Their labours not only must have illuminated the spiritual lives of all conditions of people, but also must have prepared the kingdoms for the political unifications which led to the making of Scotland.

The first union was that of the Scots and the Picts, under Kenneth mac Alpin, King of Scots, in 843. Thenceforward, the united kingdom ruled by Kenneth and his descendants was called 'Scotia', and its old Irish name of 'Alba' or 'Albainn' survived in that of the later Scottish dukedom of Albany.

The law of succession among the Picts was matrilineal, and therefore it is presumed that the marriage of a Pictish princess into the Royal House of Dal Riata gave Kenneth mac Alpin his claim to the kingship of the Picts. Kenneth was remembered as having been a man of 'marvellous astuteness'; but he was probably also a man of extraordinary ruthlessness. Apparently in consequence of the union of the two peoples, the Picts disappeared, and whatever records they may have had were consigned to oblivion. Kenneth may have forced his rule upon the Picts by defeating them in battle, but the twelfth-century historian Giraldus Cambrensis recalled a darker story in which Kenneth had secured the ascendancy of the Scots by ordering a massacre of the Pictish nobility.

Yet even so savage a measure would scarcely explain the total destruction of Pictish culture which followed Kenneth's accession. A possible explanation is that the destruction of the Picts was largely the consequence of warfare with the Norsemen, for the union of the Scots and Picts occurred just as the whole of Britain was enduring the Viking invasions.

The Vikings came first to plunder but remained to settle. Orkney, Shetland and the Western Isles remained Norse-dominated for centuries. Permanent settlements were also made on the west coast of Scotia, and as far south as Cumbria. The Vikings arrived as pagans, but gradually adopted Christianity. The doubtful quality of some of their conversions is well illustrated by an incident recounted in the *Orkneyinga Saga*. King Olaf Tryggvason, who ruled Norway from 995 to 1000, when recently converted, visited his vassal, Earl Sigurd of Orkney. Summoning Sigurd on board his ship, Olaf said to him, 'I want you and all your subjects to be baptized. If you refuse I'll have you killed on the spot, and I swear I'll ravage every island with fire and steel.'* The Orcadians prudently turned Christian, but they do not appear to have received any further religious instruction at the time. However, in the following century Orkney produced a great saint, the martyr Earl Magnus, whose magnificent monument is his cathedral at Kirkwall.

In the meantime, just over twenty years after the union of the Scots and Picts, the Vikings captured York. The country to the north of it was cut off from the rest of Anglo-Saxon England, leaving it a debatable land which successive kings of Scotia aspired to add to their kingdom. Kenneth mac Alpin himself is said to have invaded it six times, while failing to conquer it. The annexation of Lothian, and additional territories to the south of it, continued to preoccupy his successors.

Although matrilinearism had probably provided Kenneth mac Alpin with a pretext for securing the Pictish throne, this custom, together with the rest of Pictish culture, disappeared. Succession to the kingship of Scotia, as to that of Dal Riata, was decided by

*trans. Hermann Pálsson and Paul Edwards.

tanistry. According to this system the king had to be a member of the *derbfine*, or 'certain kin', which comprised four generations descended from a common ancestor who had been a king. Any male member of the *derbfine* could be accepted as king, provided he was recognizably *rígdomnae* – 'the stuff of kings'. In the hope, usually vain, that eligible kinsmen would not fight among themselves, a strong king would nominate his successor during his lifetime. The successor, who gave the system its name, was the tanist: the *tanaise ríg*, which meant 'second to the king'. Kenneth mac Alpin himself, while he was certainly a descendant of Fergus Mor mac Erc, was the son of a man who is believed not to have been a king. Probably he became King of Scots by the exercise of just such ruthlessness as the tanistry system encouraged.

The system decided the succession to the throne of Scotia for the next two centuries. How it worked in practice may be seen in the following table:

Kenneth I mac Alpin, 843–59
Donald I, 859–63 (brother of Kenneth)
Constantine I, 863–77 (elder son of Kenneth)
Aed, 877–8 (younger son of Kenneth)
Eochaid, 878–89 (nephew of Aed)
Donald II, 889–900 (son of Constantine I)
Constantine II, 900–42 (son of Aed)
Malcolm I, 942–54 (son of Donald II)
Indulf, 954–62 (son of Constantine II)
Dubh, 962–7 (elder son of Malcolm I)
Cuilean, 967–71 (son of Indulf)
Kenneth II, 971–95 (younger son of Malcolm I)
Constantine III, 995–7 (son of Cuilean)
Kenneth III, 997–1005 (son of Dubh)
Malcolm II, 1005–34 (son of Kenneth II)

Though the succession may appear to have been tossed upon the storms of ambition, it was firmly confined within the *derbfine*. Malcolm II, the last of this dynasty, was the great-great-great-great-grandson of Kenneth mac Alpin.

Most of the kings of the House of Alpin are only names, for insufficient evidence survives to suggest their characters. But during their reigns certain events occurred which decisively influenced the future development of Scotland.

Kenneth mac Alpin himself, seeking both to strengthen his hold upon the former territory of the Picts, and yielding before the pressure of the Viking attacks on the coast of Dal Riata, established his seat of government at Scone, which was to become the coronation place of the Scottish kings. To Scone he brought the palladium of the Scots, the *Lía Fail*, or 'Stone of Destiny', which in time came to be called the 'Stone of Scone'. The Kings of Scots were ceremonially seated upon the sacred stone as part of the ritual of their inauguration. Obviously this action was a survival from the pagan past, but Christian legend had biblicalized the stone itself, by claiming that it was the stone which had been Jacob's pillow at Bethel, carried thence to Ireland by remote ancestors of the Scots, and brought to Dal Riata by Fergus Mor mac Erc.

Kenneth mac Alpin also moved the spiritual centre of the country from Iona, which was sacked by the Vikings, to Dunkeld, to which he brought the relics of St Columba. In 943 they were moved again by Constantine II, who abdicated to enter the monastery of St Andrews taking the precious relics with him. Iona always remained a sacred place, as many centuries later Dr Johnson recognized when he said that 'man is little to be envied whose patriotism would not gain force upon the plain of Marathon, or whose piety would not grow warmer among the ruins of Iona'.

St Andrews in time became the new spiritual capital, and in the late fifteenth century, during the reign of James III it became the primatial see of Scotland. But, though legends gave it an almost certainly spurious connection with the apostle, whose relics were supposed to have been brought there by St Rule, it owed its original numinosity to the presence of the relics of St Columba.

While St Andrews gained in importance, Edinburgh, the future capital, still lay outside the Kingdom of Scotia, in the Anglian enclave of Lothian. The great rock of Edinburgh was captured by King Indulf, but the rest of Lothian remained unconquered until Malcolm II was able to annex it after his victory at Carham-on-Tweed, in 1018.

Malcolm II was a powerful and successful ruler who reigned for almost thirty years and was over eighty when he died. His grandson, Duncan, became King of Strathclyde, as the last of a line of Scottish sub-kings who ruled Strathclyde as a dependency of Scotia. When Malcolm died in 1034 Duncan succeeded him, and united Strathclyde to Scotia and Lothian. Though the Western Isles were not recovered from Norse rule until the thirteenth century, nor Orkney and Shetland until the fifteenth, and though the frontier with England long remained fluid, the four kingdoms of North Britain had recognizably become Scotland.

CHAPTER TWO

The Kingdom of the Scots
1034 – 1286

Historically the most important fact about Duncan I is that he was the first King of Scots to rule over the unified mainland of Scotland, but perversely, the best known fact about him is that he was slain by Macbeth. Shakespeare's *Macbeth* makes this episode of Scottish history appear to stand out from the immediate past with extraordinary clarity, but the drama owes its splendour to Shakespeare's imagination, and the plot, derived from Holinshed's semi-fictitious *Chronicle*, falsifies the facts.

Malcolm II obviously nominated Duncan as his successor because Duncan was already King of Strathclyde, so that his accession would unite the four kingdoms – a policy in conformity with the traditional ambitions of the House of Alpin. But equally traditional was strife among the royal kinsmen, and in this context Macbeth's ambition to displace Duncan was not in itself treasonable.

Duncan and Macbeth were first cousins. Duncan was the son of Malcolm II's elder daughter Bethoc, by her husband Crinan, lay-abbot of Dunkeld; Macbeth was the son of Malcolm's younger daughter by her husband Findlaech, *Mormaer* of Moray. (*Mormaer* was a Celtic title, but whether it was hereditary or official is controversial.) The historical Lady Macbeth was Gruoch, a granddaughter of King Kenneth III, who may well have encouraged Macbeth to assert his claim to the throne, which in her eyes would have been lawful.

In 1040 Macbeth defeated and slew Duncan in battle, and made himself King. By 1050 he was secure enough to make a pilgrimage to Rome, where with the piety of his period he 'scattered money among the poor like seed'. Macbeth was overthrown when Duncan's sons, children at the time of their father's death, reached maturity. Duncan's sons, Malcolm and Donald *Ban* (Shakespeare's Donalbain, whose Gaelic nickname means 'the Fair' or 'the White'), had been sent to England and Ireland respectively, for safety during Macbeth's reign. Their 'separated fortune' to which Shakespeare correctly referred, led naturally to separate ambitions, and ultimately to enmity between them.

With English support Malcolm invaded Scotland in 1057, and defeated Macbeth who was killed in battle at Lumphanan in Aberdeenshire. Malcolm gained the throne by the same means as Macbeth, but the dynasty which he successfully established, the House of Dunkeld (deriving its name from the abbacy of Dunkeld held by Duncan I's father), adopted succession by primogeniture, a more satisfactory system than tanistry, with its repeated blood-letting.

Malcolm III was known as *Ceann-Mor*, or 'Great Chief', a nickname which doubtless conveys exactly what he was. Though he remained illiterate all his life he proved himself capable of responding to civilizing influences. The most far-reaching of these resulted from the Norman Conquest of England in 1066, which threw upon Malcolm's mercy the fugitive members of the Anglo-Saxon royal house, including Edgar the

Atheling, or heir to the throne, and his sister Margaret. They were the children of Edward the Exile, grandson of King Ethelred II. When the Danish King Canute made himself King of England, Edward the Exile fled to Hungary, where he married a German princess. The children of this union spent their early years in Hungary, during the generation after its conversion to Christianity. In 1057 they were brought to England, to live at the court of Edward the Confessor, which was already permeated by Norman-French influences, which the English resented and feared with good reason.

In 1069 Malcolm III married Margaret as his second wife. His first marriage had been with Ingibiorg of Orkney, an alliance which linked him with Scandinavia. His marriage with Margaret exposed him and his kingdom to new cultural and political influences, for Margaret, with the broad experience of her cosmopolitan background, brought to Scotland a first intimation of the flowering of medieval Europe. In character Margaret was ascetic, devout and civilized, and for her virtues and her devotion to the Church she was canonized in 1250. She inspired in Malcolm a lifelong and unwavering love, which was the foundation of her influence on his kingdom. Margaret's confessor Turgot wrote an account of her life which contains a remarkable description of Malcolm's devotion:

He readily obeyed her wishes and prudent counsels in all things. Whatever she refused, he refused also; whatever pleased her he also loved for love of her. Hence it was that although he could not read, he would turn over and examine books which she used either for her devotions or her study; and whenever he heard her express liking for a particular book, he would also look at it with special interest, kissing it and often taking it into his hands. Sometimes he sent for a worker in precious metals, whom he commanded to ornament that volume with gold and gems, and when the work was finished the King himself used to carry the book to the Queen as a loving proof of his devotion.

To the Scottish court, which had resembled that of a tribal chief rather than that of a European king, Margaret brought good manners, which are always a touchstone of civilization, and a more elaborate use of ceremonial, which served to enhance the prestige of Scotland in its contacts with the greater powers of Christendom.

While Margaret possessed a strong sense of regality, her piety led her to interest herself particularly in religious affairs. She founded the Benedictine Priory of Dunfermline, by the importation of Benedictine monks from Canterbury, and in conjunction with Malcolm she granted an endowment to the Culdee community of Lochleven. (The Culdees were Celtic monks whose original name *Celi Dé* meant 'Companions of God'.) Yet Margaret has often been represented as the enemy of the Celtic Church, as though 'Celtic' and 'Roman' were as opposed as 'Protestant' and 'Catholic' were to be in later times.

The reality of the situation was that Margaret found Scotland still in a period of readjustment after the triumph of the Roman system over the divergent organization of Christian life in Celtic society. The Celtic Church, out of touch with Rome after the downfall of the Roman Empire, remained long unaware of the reforms of the liturgical calendar which had twice affected the official method of calculating the date of Easter. This may now seem unimportant, but while the Church was still converting pagans on the fringes of Europe, disagreement among Christians concerning the date of the greatest event of the Christian year could cast doubt upon the credibility of missionaries. It was necessary to reach agreement.

Other differences were entirely organizational. Under the late Roman Empire, with its many cities, provincial capitals had become episcopal sees, and a diocesan and parochial structure had been easily developed. In the thinly populated Celtic lands, as in the Egyptian desert whence it derived, monasticism had seemed the appropriate expression of the Christian life. In the aristocratic societies of Ireland, Scottish Dal Riata, and the Kingdom of the Picts, monasticism took root, with royally related abbots like St Columba exercising the principal authority, while the function of bishops, who were less socially conspicuous, was chiefly sacramental.

In 663, at the Synod of Whitby, the Celtic Church of Northumbria accepted the Roman Calendar, followed by the Picts, then by Iona in 716, and thereafter by Ireland. By the time that Margaret's influence was brought to bear in Scotland the outstanding Celtic-Roman differences had been resolved; fortunately there had been no doctrinal divergences. What remained to attract Margaret's reforming zeal were local abuses: clerical marriage, the celebration of Mass in the vernacular, and the widespread habit of receiving Communion very infrequently. In bringing Scottish practices into line with the mainstream of

Christendom, Margaret had the strong support of Malcolm.

Though Malcolm followed his wife's judgement in religious matters, politically he imitated his predecessors. Like them, he was determined to push his frontier with England further south. Championship of his brother-in-law Edgar the *Atheling* provided an excuse for repeated invasions. But William the Conqueror was an ill-chosen adversary. In 1072 he led an army into Scotland, either to do battle or to warn Malcolm against further interference. Malcolm recognized William's military superiority, and received him peaceably at Abernethy, where he took an oath to be 'his man'. This politic act of homage saved the immediate situation but stored up trouble for the future, since it opened the question of Scotland's status *vis-à-vis* England, which was to embitter Anglo-Scottish relations. In the meantime William returned south, taking as a hostage Duncan, Malcolm's son by Ingibiorg.

Malcolm was not deterred from expansionism, but Duncan's life was not exacted; England had another use for him. In 1093 Malcolm and the eldest of his six sons by Margaret were ambushed and killed at Alnwick, at the outset of a fifth invasion of England. Margaret, who was already mortally ill, died in Edinburgh Castle on receiving the news of their deaths.

The reforms of Malcolm and Margaret in court and Church, and the accompanying changes in the character of society, had been acceptable in the Lowlands, but beyond the Highland Line these innovations had been ill-regarded. The deaths of the King and Queen provoked an immediate Celtic reaction, led by Donald *Ban*, an ageing but undaunted aspirant to the throne.

The bereaved sons of Malcolm and Margaret were unprepared for the appearance of his forces before the walls of Edinburgh Castle. They abandoned the defences, carried the body of their mother to Dunfermline for burial, and fled to England.

William Rufus, the Conqueror's son and successor, had excellent reasons for welcoming them. Since England held their half-brother, Duncan, hostage, now he could be assisted to the Scottish throne as a grateful vassal, without their resistance. In 1094 William Rufus provided an army with which Duncan overthrew Donald *Ban*, and proclaimed himself Duncan II. But his tenure of power was brief. Duncan II was soon murdered and Donald *Ban* restored. William Rufus then offered his assistance to Edgar, the son of Malcolm and Margaret, who in 1097, with an Anglo-Norman army defeated Donald *Ban*, who was imprisoned and blinded.

Edgar, despite his savage treatment of his predecessor, was known as Edgar 'the Peaceable', a name which may not have been bestowed for complimentary reasons. In 1098 he formally ceded the Western Isles to Magnus Barelegs, King of Norway, in recognition of the long-established Norse occupation which he lacked the strength to dislodge. On Edgar's death without issue in 1107, he was succeeded by his brother Alexander I, 'the Fierce', a more forceful character who was described as ruling his kingdom *laboriossissime* – 'with a great deal of hard work' – which included the quelling of a rebellion in Moray, the province of Macbeth, and the defence of the Church in Scotland against claims to metropolitan authority by the Archbishops of York. (This question was not resolved until 1192, when Pope Celestine III declared the Church in Scotland to be under the direct authority and protection of Rome.)

Alexander I, who married a daughter of Henry I of England, died childless in 1124, to be succeeded by the youngest of Malcolm and Margaret's sons, David I, who proved to be the greatest of his family. King David also married an English wife, Matilda of Huntingdon, an heiress who brought him vast territories in the English Midlands. Under Edgar, Alexander I and David I Scotland enjoyed stable and effective government, and the friendly relations which the three kings successively maintained with William Rufus and Henry I probably saved Scotland from a renewed threat of Anglo-Norman conquest, which an aggressive policy like that of Malcolm *Ceann-Mor* would have been likely to provoke.

When Henry I died in 1135 David reverted to this policy, seeking to take advantage of the civil war which broke out in England between Henry's daughter Maud and his nephew Stephen. David's advance into England was checked in 1138 by a defeat at the Battle of the Standard, near Northallerton, in Yorkshire. But Stephen was too hard-pressed elsewhere to take advantage of the event, so that by the Treaty of Durham in 1139 the whole of Northumbria, except the fortresses of Newcastle and Bamburgh, was ceded to David's son, Earl Henry, and so became Scottish territory. This proved to be a temporary gain.

David I's more lasting work lay in his own kingdom. During the reigns of his brothers there had been some peaceful Anglo-Norman infiltration of Scotland by individuals seeking advancement which they had failed to win under their own kings. David I converted a trend into a policy. In his own contacts with England

David had been impressed by the efficiency of the feudal system introduced by William the Conqueror and his successors. Simply expressed, the underlying theory was that all land belonged to the king: tenants-in-chief held their land directly from the king in return for political support and military service; sub-tenants held from tenants-in-chief in return for military service, and the whole structure was held together by the oath of homage which each man paid to his feudal superior. The unfree peasantry worked the land, and in return for providing the basic sustenance of society, received security and protection. This comprehensive system of obligation and benefit worked imperfectly, as do all human institutions, but under a strong king it could provide the framework of a prosperous and efficient kingdom.

David I saw the advantage of a system which could convert the King of Scots from a partly Europeanized chief like his father into a feudal king, and he had the means to effect the change by importing Anglo-Norman knights from his English lands as the feudal superiors of small landholders in Scotland. (The fortunes of the future royal families of Balliol, Bruce and Stewart, whose remote ancestors were respectively Picard, Norman and Breton, were made by this means.) Most of King David's feudalization was introduced south of the Forth-Clyde line, but he was able to extend it into Moray by converting the *Mormaers* and their subordinate *Toiseachs* into earls and barons, and their tribal followers into feudal tenants.

His court took on a more cosmopolitan structure with the introduction of the great officials – Butler, Chamberlain, Chancellor, Constable, Marshal and

Steward – which characterized the courts of medieval Europe. His immense energy affected every aspect of society. Not only did he establish the first Royal Burghs, towns which in return for an annual payment to the king were permitted to conduct foreign trade, he also endeavoured to establish a uniform legal system throughout the kingdom; he instituted the first consistent system of weights and measures, and he issued the first Scottish coinage. In the course of David's reign the loose organization of Celtic society was converted into the close structure of a relatively efficient feudal kingdom. The significance of David's achievement was that it saved Scotland from the unhappy fate which overtook Wales and Ireland, where a similar metamorphosis had not taken place, under the stress of English aggression.

In religious matters David inherited the zeal of his mother, which he expressed by intensified importation of European monasticism. He founded four communities of Cistercians at Melrose, Dundrennan, Newbattle and Kinloss; five communities of Augustinian canons, at Holyrood, Jedburgh, Cambuskenneth, and on St Serf's Island in Lochleven; and he established Tironensians at Kelso, Premonstratensians at Dryburgh, and Cluniacs on the Isle of May. One of David's successors, finding the resources of the Crown depleted, bitterly referred to him as 'ane sair sanct for the Crown'; but David I did not impoverish the Crown to endow the Church, as the prosperity of his immediate successors proved. Moreover, his foundations benefited the kingdom, for monasteries were not only houses of prayer, they were centres of social service, for they provided the only schools, they dispensed charity and gave medical care, and they pioneered new methods of agriculture.

David I died in 1153, predeceased by his promising son, Earl Henry. His successor was his eleven-year-old grandson, Malcolm IV. The boy King grew up to be an extraordinarily holy young man, 'a terrestrial angel', in the opinion of a contemporary. He took a vow of chastity, to the disapproval of his mother, Ada de Varenne, who is said to have arranged dissuasive temptations; but he persevered, and died as chaste as he had lived. Posterity remembered him as 'Malcolm the Maiden'.

The year after Malcolm's accession, Stephen of England was succeeded by the rapaciously ambitious Henry II, the first king of the Plantagenet dynasty which continually threatened Scotland's independence. In 1157 Henry II met King Malcolm at Chester and demanded the restitution of the territory which Stephen had ceded to David I's son. Malcolm lacked both the resources and the experience to resist. In his own kingdom, however, his rule was successful. He was strong enough to quell separatist rebellions in Argyll, Moray and Galloway; probably he owed his success to the reservoir of loyalty provided by his grandfather's imported tenants-in-chief. Thus encouraged he continued David I's policy of feudalization, not only from his English lands, a source which may have been reaching exhaustion, but by general invitation, in which he was imitated by his brother William 'the Lion', who succeeded him in 1165.

William was obsessed by the loss of Northumbria, and influenced by the expansionist ambitions of his predecessors. An opportunity to invade northern England was offered when Henry II was in difficulties after the murder of Thomas Becket. In 1174, when Henry's turbulent sons were in revolt against him, William captured several English strongholds before he was ambushed and taken prisoner at Alnwick, the ill-omened place where Malcolm *Ceann-Mor* had met his death. Henry II had William transported to Falaise in Normandy, where he was compelled to acknowledge Henry as overlord of Scotland, and to procure his release with a formal act of homage for his kingdom to which he was permitted to return the following year.

William the Lion remained the vassal of the English King until Henry II's death. But in 1189 Henry's son Richard *Coeur de Lion* was more interested in raising money for the Third Crusade than in maintaining his overlordship of Scotland. For a payment of 10,000 merks Richard restored William to full sovereignty by an agreement known as the 'Quitclaim of Canterbury'. According to the contemporary chronicler Roger Howden, William paid homage to Richard for 'the holding of his dignities in England', and 'King Richard quit claimed him and all his heirs forever ... from all allegiance and subjection for the Kingdom of Scotland.' It was an agreement clear enough to have settled the matter.

The whole question of homage owed by one king to another for lands held in a neighbouring kingdom was fraught with tension and resentment. No king enjoyed being seen on his knees before another, for the ritual appeared to jeopardize his status; yet no king wanted to yield any lands which he felt were his by right. The kings of England held lands in France for which they were obliged, and reluctant, to pay homage to the French kings. Feudal society was a tissue of such obligations.

William the Lion died in 1214, after a reign of nearly forty-nine years. He had been fifty-six when his Queen, Ermengarde de Beaumont, bore him a son in 1198. He was fortunate in living long enough to see his late-born heir, who was named Alexander, develop into a mature and promising prince. Anglo-Scottish relations had remained reasonably amicable during the later years of William the Lion, but the accession of the sixteen-year-old Alexander II aroused the ambitions of King John, who declared that he intended to 'hunt the red fox cub from his den'. This was a genuine reference to Alexander II's appearance, as John had received him at the English court and knighted him, in 1212. However, Alexander was as foxy in character as in colouring, for he took the initiative against King John, by supporting the English barons who forced Magna Carta on their reluctant King in 1215.

After John's death better relations between the two kingdoms were restored, and in 1221 Alexander married Joanna, the sister of the young King Henry III. In 1236 the two Kings met at York, to resolve outstanding disputes between Scotland and England, and they agreed that the Tweed-Solway line should be the frontier of their kingdoms. Two years later Alexander's English Queen died without issue, and in 1239 he married Marie de Coucy, the daughter of a great French baron, Enguerrand de Coucy, who defined his position in the feudal world with an arrogant rhymed motto:

Ni Roy, ni Prince, ni Duc, je suis,
Je suis le Seigneur de Coucy

In 1241 Queen Marie bore her husband their only

child, which fortunately was a son. This prince, Alexander, who was to reign with honour, and die lamented for centuries, succeeded when he was eight years old. The inauguration of Alexander III has aroused great interest, because he was the last king of the House of Dunkeld, and his inauguration was a very ancient ritual, unlike the coronation ceremonies of other medieval kings.

The boy King was brought to Scone and enthroned out of doors, beside a cross in the churchyard, on the sacred stone of the Scots, which the chronicler Walter of Guisborough described as 'large, concave, and shaped like a round chair'. When the King was enthroned his nobles knelt before him and cast their cloaks on the ground. Then a Highland *seannachie*, or bard, declaimed in Gaelic the King's genealogy, extending beyond Fergus Mor mac Erc to the mythical Fergus, son of Ferehard, and further again to the eponymous matriarch of the Scots, Scota, daughter of the Pharaoh from whom the Israelites had fled. The ceremony included neither crowning nor anointing, though Alexander III wore a crown and carried a sceptre, probably introduced as status symbols, necessary to assert the equality of the King of Scots with the King of England, and to impress it upon the more recently established tenants-in-chief.

When Alexander was only ten years old he was married to Margaret, daughter of Henry III of England. Even at so early an age, when he paid homage to his father-in-law for the lands he held in England, Alexander was shrewd enough to avoid being trapped into paying homage for his own kingdom. In 1272 Henry III died, and once again Alexander was obliged to renew his homage for his English lands, to the new

King, his brother-in-law, Edward I. He paid it with the stern reminder that so far as homage for Scotland was concerned, 'to that none has a right, save God alone'.

Edward I recognized the strength of character of Alexander III, and respected his sovereignty. But it was an ill omen for the future that the status of Scotland was protected not by the provisions of the Quitclaim of Canterbury but by the personality of the king. In retrospect, the years between 1189, in which the Quitclaim was negotiated, and 1286, in which Alexander died, made up almost a century of borrowed time. During that period the ambitions of successive Plantagenet kings, John, Henry III and Edward I, had been occasionally revealed, and successfully countered; but the unhappy political truth that an agreement is worth nothing if it cannot be defended with force would be proved after the death of Alexander III.

In the meantime, the event which most impressively symbolized the success of Alexander's reign was the recovery of the Western Isles. In 1263 Haakon the Old, King of Norway, brought a great fleet to the west coast, to defend Norwegian possession, and in October he was defeated at the Battle of Largs, by a combination of Scottish sea power and autumnal gales. He withdrew his battered fleet to Orkney, where he died. In 1266 the Western Isles were formally ceded to Scotland by the Treaty of Perth.

During the next twenty years, under Alexander III's strong rule, Scotland enjoyed peace and prosperity. The 'Norman Conquest by invitation' which had taken place under David I, Malcolm IV and William the Lion, was finally absorbed and Scotticized. Anglo-Norman, Norman, French and Flemish tenants-in-chief and sub-tenants had been established as far north as Aberdeenshire, Moray and Sutherland, and to the south-west in Ayrshire and Dumfriesshire. At first they formed a French-speaking aristocracy, delighting in their own inheritance of chivalric romances, which inspired them to call Edinburgh 'Tanebroc', its castle, which was sometimes known as 'The Maidens' Castle', 'La Chastel des Pucelles', Roxburgh 'Le March Mont' (thus giving rise to its alternative name of Marchmont), and so on. Under this influence Lachlan, Lord of Galloway, was somewhat absurdly inspired to re-christen himself Roland. But soon the influence was reversed, and the incomers abandoned their own language in favour of the Anglian-based Scots vernacular which, by the mid-thirteenth century was widely spoken throughout the Lowlands. Gaelic, originating in Ireland, which had been the language of the Scots of Dal Riata, had probably spread throughout a great part of the former Kingdom of the Picts, under the kings of the House of Alpin. The linguistic turn of the tide in favour of Scots was slow, but by the end of the thirteenth century Scots was probably spoken throughout almost the whole area south-east of the Highland Line.

The growth of town life, an economic phenomenon which exclusively affected the Lowlands, encouraged the same trend. The east coast ports enjoyed a flourishing trade with England and Flanders, while Perth, which was accessible to the seagoing vessels of the period, shared this prosperity, and became for a time the principal city of the kingdom. The use of the mutually comprehensible Scots and English tongues by the trading communities made its own contribution to the decline of Gaelic outside the Highlands.

However, linguistic dichotomy did not at this period imply hostility, as later it came to do. Gaels, Lowlanders and naturalized incomers, united in their loyalty to a strong and beloved King, in the late thirteenth century became the Scots, whose sense of a common identity gave them the strength to resist the troubles which beset the kingdom as the century approached its end.

Fortune deserted Alexander III before it deserted Scotland. In 1275 Queen Margaret died, but it appeared that the succession was secure, for she had borne three children, Margaret, Alexander and David. Margaret married Erik II of Norway in 1281, and two years later died, leaving a daughter who was also named Margaret. Then David died in 1281 and Alexander in 1284, so that the royal line was represented only by the King's granddaughter in Norway.

In 1285 Alexander III remarried, in the hope of begetting another son. His second wife was Yolande, daughter of the Comte de Dreux, said to have been 'the fairest of women'. Whether passion or anxiety urged him the more, the King left a Council of his Lords in Edinburgh Castle, on a wild night in March 1286, to cross the Firth of Forth to Kinghorn, where the Queen awaited him. He crossed the Forth in safety, but as he rode through the darkness along the north shore his horse missed its footing on the cliff path and flung the King to his death on the rocks below. The Queen bore no child, and the darkness and tragedy of that night seemed imprinted upon the Kingdom of the Scots for many years to come.

CHAPTER THREE

A Kingdom Becomes a Nation
1286 – 1371

A fragment of medieval verse captures the regret with which the Scots remembered their great King's reign:

> When Alysandyr our King was dede
>   That Scotland held in love and le /law/,
> Away was sons /plenty/ of ale and brede,
>   Of wine and wax, of game and glee;
> Our gold was changit into lede.
>   Christ, borne into Virginité,
> Succour Scotland, and remede,
>   That stad is in perplexité

In that verse the benefits of Alexander III's reign are captured in simple words: 'love and law' and 'game and glee'. He was a great ruler indeed who could impose law and maintain it by love, and whose subjects had the time and the spirit to include 'game and glee' in their lives.

Though his great presence was removed, it did not seem at first that the status of the kingdom would be threatened. During Alexander's lifetime his grand-daughter Margaret had been recognized as his heiress. Margaret, the 'Maid of Norway', was born in 1283 and so she was three years old when her grandfather met his death. The Maid of Norway was immediately acknowledged as 'Lady and Queen' of Scotland, and six Guardians were appointed to govern the kingdom during her minority. They soon received from Edward I of England a proposal of marriage between Margaret and his son Edward of Caernarvon, who had been born in 1284. The Guardians of Scotland were sufficiently mindful of past history to receive the English proposal with caution. By the Treaty of Salisbury of 1289 and the Treaty of Burgham of 1290 it was agreed that the Queen of Scotland should marry the heir of England, but that the 'rights, laws, liberties and customs of Scotland' should be 'wholly and inviolably preserved', and that Scotland should remain 'separate and divided from the Kingdom of England'.

While Edward I had not presumed to trespass upon the sovereign rights of the strong King Alexander III, doubtless his ambition to extend his authority over Scotland had at least taken shape in his mind when the marriage of the two children was planned. Scotland might be expected to become subordinate to England, just as the wife was expected to become subordinate to the husband, despite the careful provisions which the Guardians wrote into the treaties. A vaguely threatening situation became infinitely dangerous when the little Queen Margaret died in May 1290, leaving Scotland a disputed succession of unexampled complexity.

There were thirteen claimants to the throne, resulting from the fact that the House of Dunkeld had ended in the male line with the death of Alexander III, and the direct succession in the female line with the death of his granddaughter. However, Malcolm the Maiden and William the Lion had had a younger brother, David, Earl of Huntingdon, who had three daughters,

Margaret, Isabella and Ada. Margaret had married Alan, Lord of Galloway, and their daughter Dervorguilla married John Balliol, a nobleman of Picard descent, whose family had been established in Scotland by David I. Isabella had married Robert Bruce (or de Brus) whose family came from Brix near Cherbourg, and also owed its advancement to King David. Ada married an Anglo-Norman nobleman named Henry de Hastings. The descendants of these three marriages provided the principal claimants.

John Balliol the younger, son of Dervorguilla and her husband, had the best claim in strict primogeniture. Robert Bruce of Annandale contested the claim on two counts: first, that he was the grandson of Earl David, whereas the younger Balliol was the great-grandson, and therefore at one further remove from royalty; and second, that Alexander II, while still childless, had designated Bruce as his heir. Lord Hastings, the descendant of Ada, argued that Earl David's three daughters ought to be regarded as co-heiresses, and Scotland as a fief of England, which should be divided between Balliol, Bruce and himself. This was a forlorn hope, as even kingdoms which were undoubtedly subordinate to others were not regarded as divisible under feudal law. Scotland, though its status had at one time been subordinate, certainly did not fall into the divisible category. The remaining claimants represented even more forlorn hopes.

The claimants, who are often known as the 'Competitors' – a name which no doubt accurately conveys their state of mind – resolved to submit their disputes to the arbitration of Edward I. With the benefit of hindsight it appears that they were among those whom the gods wish to destroy, and accordingly first make mad. But it must be remembered that when they submitted their dispute to Edward I they knew him only as the brother-in-law of their late King, and as the neighbouring sovereign who had accepted the stipulations of the treaties concerning the future status of Scotland. Posterity was to know Edward as the 'Hammer of the Scots'; so far, these contemporaries did not.

Edward I deliberated with every appearance of impartiality, and decided, with scrupulous correctness, in favour of John Balliol. He gave his decision in the great hall of Berwick Castle on 17 November 1292. Before giving his judgement Edward had demanded that the Competitors should acknowledge him as their feudal superior, and this demand had not awakened their suspicions: he was a king, and they were not, and some of them, including Balliol and Bruce, held lands from him in England. No doubt it would have seemed a reasonable demand, merely to secure the acceptance of his final decision. But, the decision once made, the trap was sprung. Edward then demanded that Balliol, now recognized as King of Scots, should renew his oath of homage, and Balliol was in no position to refuse, for to refuse would have been to reassert the independence of Scotland, which he could not do, because he lacked the support of the other Competitors for the Crown. The humiliated Balliol renewed his homage to Edward, and on the last day of November, St Andrew's Day, he was inaugurated as King of Scots, and enthroned upon the sacred stone at Scone. He then accompanied King Edward to England, and at Newcastle on 26 December he did homage for Scotland.

Edward's ambition, hitherto veiled by the forms of

legality, was not satisfied. It was soon revealed as nothing less than the conquest of Scotland. The age-old English urge to dominate the northern king-dom might appear dormant when the King of Scots was strong, but it would always awake again when the King of Scots was weak. Edward I, one of the most forceful kings of the Plantagenet dynasty, now had an opportunity of which he made the most. Still keeping within the letter of the law, but distorting the spirit of feudalism, Edward made the pressure of English overlordship intolerable. He calculated that it would be only a matter of time before Balliol was driven to revolt, then he could be crushed as a rebel, and the conquest of Scotland could be disguised as the reimposition of lawful authority.

Balliol was summoned to provide military support in France, where Edward I was fighting the French King Philip IV (to whom he himself owed homage for his English lands in France). Yet more humiliating were summonses to Balliol to appear in English courts to answer complaints and appeals by his own subjects. As Edward had intended, Balliol's uncertain authority was so much undermined that his position became unendurable. His response may have been predictable, but it was not undignified. In 1295 he repudiated his allegiance to Edward I, and made a treaty of alliance with France. This was the first of a series of Franco-Scottish treaties which bound Scotland and France together in the long bond of the auld alliance which continued as a political relationship until the sixteenth century, and thereafter as a tradition of friendship.

Edward I's premeditated retaliation was terrible in its effect. In 1296 he invaded Scotland and sacked Berwick, the kingdom's most prosperous port. He massacred the inhabitants without regard to their sex or age, and then marched on to defeat John Balliol's army, near Dunbar. On 11 July, at Brechin, Balliol was forced to surrender his kingdom. He was stripped of the trappings of his regality, and sent to captivity in the Tower of London.

When Edward himself returned to England he endeavoured to symbolize the extinction of the Kingdom of the Scots by taking with him the sacred stone of Scone. In this symbolic action he may have been outwitted, for the unremarkable block of sandstone lodged in the coronation chair in Westminster Abbey has been identified by geologists as originating in the neighbourhood of Scone. The sacred stone, even if it had not been brought from the Middle East, might at least have betrayed an origin in Irish Dal Riata. Furthermore, Edward's trophy was certainly not large, concave, and shaped like a round chair, as Walter of Guisborough had described the sacred stone.

In 1296 Edward I aroused the very passions which his actions had been calculated to destroy. The Kingdom of the Scots refused to accept extinction, and since it was a kingdom without a king, its sense of identity was forced to seek a new form of expression, that of nationhood. Edward I's hammering of the Scots did not serve his own intention of hammering them into submission; rather, it forged a sense of nationality so strong that neither the Union of Crowns in 1603 nor the Union of Parliaments in 1707 served to make the United Kingdom much more than a geographical expression. At the death of Alexander III Scotland had been a small kingdom of Christendom, occupied by the Scots; in the ensuing decade it discovered itself to be a nation composed of Scots who were not content to be metamorphosed into Englishmen.

Scotland's national self-discovery progressed during Edward's most active period of attempted conquest, and it was personified by the resistance leader, Sir William Wallace, who is justly regarded as Scotland's national hero. Though he was at his best as a guerrilla leader, Wallace nonetheless achieved a full-scale victory in September 1297, when he defeated an English army commanded by the Earl of Surrey at the Battle of Stirling Bridge. In July 1298, however, Wallace was defeated by Edward himself at the Battle of Falkirk. After his defeat, Wallace's movements are for a time uncertain, but he is believed to have gone abroad to seek French and Papal support for Scotland. After his return, in 1305, he was betrayed into English hands, taken to London, tried in Westminster Hall, and condemned to death as a traitor. Unlike many prominent Scots, Wallace had never sworn allegiance to Edward I, and therefore he was undoubtedly not a traitor but a prisoner of war. Nevertheless, he died the newly devised form of traitor's death, which was to be hanged, drawn and quartered. This barbaric form of execution involved semi-strangulation, castration, disembowelment and dismemberment; it was calculated to inflict the maximum possible agony on the victim, and to keep him conscious until the dismemberment. In the instance of Wallace, it served to give Scotland's cause the supreme advantage of a martyr.

Two years later, Edward I died while on his way to command a new campaign in Scotland. His last wish, that his body should be boiled down and his bones carried at the head of his army, was very reasonably ignored by his successor Edward II, who lacked both his father's fanaticism and his lust for conquest.

A second generation took up the war. While John Balliol lived his last years at liberty on his estates in France, a new claimant to the Scottish throne appeared: Robert Bruce, the grandson of the Bruce who had been Balliol's closest competitor. The career of the young Robert Bruce gave no intimation of the character which would develop in his maturity. Some Scots, especially the most fervent admirers of Wallace, find it hard to forget that Bruce was not always a dedicated patriot. But he belonged to the great feudal aristocracy, accustomed to holding lands in two kingdoms, for whom a clash of loyalties to conflicting overlords was a matter to be resolved in personal and not national terms. For Wallace, who had no connection with England, the conflict was more clear cut. Robert Bruce supported Edward I when Balliol revoked his allegiance, which was natural because Balliol had never won the support of the erstwhile competitors. But after the deposition of Balliol, Bruce took up the Scottish cause, probably because the claim of his own family now looked more likely to succeed.

In association with John 'the Red' Comyn, Balliol's nephew, Robert Bruce became one of the new Guardians of Scotland; but the conflicting interests of the two men proved irreconcilable. Bruce went south again, and sought a reconciliation with Edward I. He changed his mind once more after the death of Wallace, for with the resultant upsurge of Scottish patriotism he may have begun to contemplate the dangerous gamble of an attempt to win the Crown. Early in 1306 Bruce endeavoured to compose his differences with Comyn, perhaps in the hope of bargaining for his support. They arranged a secret meeting in the Greyfriars Church at Dumfries, where they no sooner met than they violently quarrelled. Bruce stabbed Comyn to death in front of the high altar; such was the inauspicious prelude to the reign of the patriot King.

Bruce was in a desperate situation, from which the ultimate gamble offered the only way of escape. Comyn had lately made his own peace with King Edward, so that his murder made future reconciliation with Edward out of the question for Bruce. Furthermore, since it was a sacrilegious murder, Bruce faced excommunication.

Robert Bruce moved before either the King of England or the Pope could act. He led his handful of supporters to Scone, and there held his inauguration as King. He lacked every regal necessity. If the sacred stone was still in Scotland either its hiding place had been forgotten or there was no time to send for it. John Balliol's crown had been sent by Edward I as an offering to the shrine of St Thomas Becket at Canterbury. Bruce was seated on a makeshift throne, and crowned with a plain gold circlet. The coronation, not the enthronement, was made the central act of the ceremony, thus setting the pattern for the future.

At the outset of the reign, however, Robert Bruce was no more than a crowned fugitive, a king without achievements, and without much hope of them. A year of defeat and flight followed his coronation. The turn of the tide was his victory over an English force at Loudon Hill in 1307. This was the event which stimulated Edward I's last invasion of Scotland and precipitated his death. Thereafter, King Robert had a lesser adversary to face, for Edward II, besides being less dedicated and less able than his father, soon became locked in a power struggle with the magnates of England who were determined to break the influence of the young King's favourite, Piers Gaveston.

King Robert used the respite to work on the double task of reconquering the Lowlands from the English, and defeating his home-grown enemies, the kindred of the murdered Comyn. In 1309 he was able to hold his first Parliament, at which he received declarations of loyalty from the nobility and clergy of Scotland. Success began to produce its own fruits, and King Robert gained more support as he won back the strongholds which had been the centres of English power. One by one, Perth, Dumfries, Linlithgow, Roxburgh and Edinburgh fell. By the spring of 1314 only Stirling remained in English hands.

The relief of Stirling became the pivot of the Anglo-Scottish struggle, when its governor, Sir Philip Moubray, promised King Robert's brother Edward Bruce that he would surrender it, unless relieved by the English, on Midsummer Day 1314. In accepting this typically medieval bargain, Edward Bruce committed his brother to battle, and Moubray his sovereign to invasion. Edward II needed to recoup his prestige, after a section of his nobility had murdered Gaveston, and forced him to swallow both his grief and the insult to his authority.

At Midsummer 1314 Edward II led an army which may have numbered twenty thousand men, to the relief of Stirling Castle, to be defeated by King Robert at the Battle of Bannockburn, the decisive battle of the first War of Independence. The battle was by no means a foregone conclusion, for though Edward II was not a good commander he was a brave man, and he did not interfere with his able generals. King Robert, with an army half the size of Edward's, won a victory which was due in great part to superior knowledge of the terrain, and to the fact that he commanded an army representative of the Scottish nation, which was well aware that it was fighting for its future existence.

John Barbour's epic poem *The Brus*, which was written towards the end of the century, puts into the mouth of the King a battlefield oration which contains the words:

> '. . . for our lives
> And for our children and our wives,
> And for our freedom and our land
> In battle we are forced to stand.'

while the English

> '. . . have come thus far
> For nought but to increase their power.'*

The outcome was that the English fled ignominiously, and in the words of a contemporary chronicler thereafter 'Robert de Brus was commonly called King of Scotland by all men because he had acquired Scotland by force of arms.'

Bannockburn was the turning point of the war, not the conclusion. King Robert still faced years of struggle to wring from England acknowledgement of Scotland's independence. He also required formal recognition by the Papacy, and the lifting of the

*trans. A.A.H. Douglas.

excommunication which he had incurred by the murder of Comyn. In 1320 a representative group of the Scottish nobility wrote a joint letter to Pope John XXII, to this effect. It is known as the 'Declaration of Arbroath' (after the Abbey at which it was signed). Its best-known passage is worth quoting, for it breathes the patriotism and the sense of nationhood which the War of Independence had called into being. King Robert was described as 'another Joshua or Maccabeus', and the Declaration continued:

> To him we are obliged and resolved to adhere in all things, both upon the account of his right and his own merit, as being the person who hath restored the people's safety in defence of their liberties. But after all, if this Prince shall leave these principles he hath so nobly pursued, and consent that we or our kingdom be subjected to the King or people of England, we will immediately endeavour to expel him, as our enemy and as the subverter both of his own and our rights, and we will make another King who will defend our liberties. For so long as there shall but one hundred of us remain alive we will never give consent to subject ourselves to the dominion of the English. For it is not glory, it is not riches, neither is it honour, but it is liberty alone that we fight and contend for, which no honest man will lose but with his life.

King Robert continued 'like another Joshua or Maccabeus' to contend for Scotland's liberty, and he and his supporters were ultimately rewarded. In 1327 Edward II of England was deposed and murdered, and the government of England was for a time in the hands of his widow, Isabella of France (who was probably accessory to the crime), and of her lover Roger Mortimer, Earl of March. In 1328 this unpopular pair negotiated with King Robert the Treaty of Northampton, which acknowledged his kingship and the independence of Scotland, and promised perpetual peace between the two kingdoms. In the autumn of the same year the Pope lifted the ban of excommunication, and addressed the King as 'Our Dearest Son, Robert, Illustrious King of Scotland'.

Robert Bruce was fortunate that he lived to see the fulfilment of all that he had striven to achieve; but his death is believed to have been the slow and terrible death of leprosy. He was a pious man on whom his guilt and excommunication had weighed heavily. Before his death he requested his faithful supporter Sir James Douglas to carry his embalmed heart into battle against the enemies of Christ, since he had never been able to fulfil the knightly ideal of going on crusade. Douglas obeyed his wish, and took the King's heart to Spain, where he carried it into battle against the Moors. After Douglas's death in this campaign the King's heart was brought back to Scotland and buried in Melrose Abbey. His tomb is in the Cathedral of Dunfermline.

The succession, though assured, was not among the greatest of King Robert's achievements. He was twice married. By his first wife, Isabella of Mar, he had a daughter, Margery, who married Walter Stewart, sixth hereditary High Steward of Scotland. Their son eventually became King Robert II, the first king of the House of Stewart. However, by his second marriage to Elizabeth de Burgh, daughter of the Earl of Ulster, the King produced a late-born son. When Robert the

Bruce died in 1329 his son, David II, succeeded at the age of five.

David's reign was a leaden echo of his father's, though at first the conditions seemed propitious. Under the provisions of the Treaty of Northampton David had been married at the age of four to Joan of the Tower, the youngest daughter of Edward II. In accordance with the privileges which King Robert had obtained from the Pope, David II was crowned and anointed in the manner of a Christian king, and the ancient inauguration ceremonies of his predecessors were formally abandoned. But unhappily the best provisions which his father could make for him could not secure him against a resurgence of English ambition.

The young King Edward III of England had resented the Treaty of Northampton, which he regarded as a betrayal of his grandfather's ambitions. In 1330 he overthrew the government of his mother and Mortimer, and soon revealed that he did not intend to be bound by the agreements which they had made. In John Balliol's son Edward, King Edward III found a man who was prepared to be made King of Scots with the status of a vassal. Edward Balliol had some Scottish support from the 'Disinherited', a group of Scottish lords who had been deprived of their lands when they chose the English side in the first War of Independence. In 1332 Balliol and his supporters invaded Scotland and defeated the forces of David II at the Battle of Dupplin Moor, near Perth. Edward Balliol followed his victory with a coronation at Scone, but before the end of the year he was driven out of the country.

Edward III, who had hitherto concealed the full

extent of his ambition, now openly came to Balliol's assistance, and in July 1333 their combined armies inflicted a heavy defeat on the Scots at Halidon Hill, near Berwick. David II and his little Queen were sent to France for safety, while his supporters fought a second War of Independence, with as much determination as William Wallace and Robert the Bruce had fought the first. It was a soul-sickening and uninspiring struggle, in that it seemed a needless recapitulation of an apparently complete achievement.

Fortunately for the Scots Edward III's ambition was deflected from Scotland by the greater scope of his ambitions in France. He had a specious claim to the French throne through his mother Isabella. His pursuit of this chimera embroiled England in the Hundred Years' War with France, and enabled the Scots to save their independence for a second time. By 1341 it was considered safe for David II and his Queen to return to Scotland, but it was not long before David was called upon to repay the help which France had given him. In August 1346 Edward III defeated the French at the Battle of Crécy. King David fulfilled the terms of the Franco-Scottish alliance and invaded England, to be defeated and captured in October at the Battle of Neville's Cross, near Durham.

At Neville's Cross, Robert Stewart, who had conducted himself creditably throughout David's childhood and absence, withdrew his troops in such good order that his support of the King was considered questionable. While David remained a prisoner in England for the next eleven years he began to believe that Robert, his heir presumptive, had treacherously deserted him. From 1346 to 1357 Robert Stewart acted as Guardian of Scotland, while David's view of him grew decreasingly charitable.

By the Treaty of Berwick in 1357, David II was released for a ransom of 100,000 merks, to be paid in ten annual instalments. The ransom was never paid in full, but the taxation which was required to raise it contributed to the constitutional development of Scotland, for consent to taxation required the cooperation of the burgesses, and their attendance at parliaments opened the way to the increasing influence of the Third Estate.

After his release from captivity David II indulged in no more heroic adventures. In the disorders which his long absence had engendered he found sufficient challenge to his abilities. Slowly, he began to achieve a return to the peace, prosperity and order which Scotland had not enjoyed since the previous century. Even two visitations of the Black Death, in 1349–50 and 1361–2, did no more than interrupt the King's achievement.

David II might have enjoyed a higher reputation if he had shown willingness to settle the succession as his subjects desired. Unfortunately, but understandably, he bore a bitter grudge against Robert Stewart, who was eight years his senior, and would remain the heir presumptive so long as David himself was childless. Robert, if not particularly competent, was popular, and he begot children with Olympian prodigality. David worked hard to rule his kingdom, reaped the ingratitude which often rewards a disciplinarian, and remained childless. David's first wife, the English Queen Joan, died in 1362, and the following year he married his mistress, Margaret Logie. This second union proving as unfruitful as the first, in 1370 David took steps to obtain a divorce, with the intention of marrying a more promisingly fertile lady, named Agnes Dunbar. But before his third marriage could take place the King died suddenly, at the age of forty-six, in February 1371.

The intense reluctance of David II to see the succession pass to Robert Stewart was revealed not only by his late attempts to beget an heir, but even more by his extraordinary diplomacy with England. In return for a remission of his ransom, David offered the recognition of an English prince as his successor. (Edward III, like Robert Stewart, had no difficulty in begetting sons.) Though David intended that the accession of an English king should neither jeopardize the integrity of the kingdom nor endanger its institutions, the Scottish Parliament steadfastly refused his proposals, and firmly stated its preference for the Stewart succession. Though King David II displayed ability for which modern historians have given him due credit, it is impossible to avoid the impression that he failed to discern the intensity of his subjects' sense of nationality, or to understand that in the course of the fourteenth century the Kingdom of the Scots had become the Scottish Nation, and was no longer the King's patrimony to be bequeathed as he chose.

CHAPTER FOUR

The Early Stewarts
1371 – 1513

The first recorded ancestor of the new Royal House of Stewart was a minor Breton noble named Alan, who was steward to the Count of Dol in the late eleventh century. Alan's son Flaald sought advancement in England in the generation following the Norman Conquest, and was granted lands on the Welsh Marches by Henry I. In Scotland the fortunes of the family were founded by Flaald's grandson Walter, one of the feudal tenants-in-chief imported by David I, who granted him the barony of Renfrew, and appointed him High Steward of Scotland. The office became hereditary in his family, giving rise to the surname of Stewart. The High Stewards were among the greatest of the Scottish nobility, and Sir Walter Stewart, the sixth holder of the office, was considered sufficiently exalted to be a worthy husband for the daughter of Robert I.

That Robert Stewart, the only son of this marriage, became King Robert II was the conclusion of a chain of unlikely events. His initial survival was almost miraculous, for he was delivered by Caesarean section from the body of Margery Bruce, who died of injuries after a fall from her horse. When he was two years old, in 1318, he was acknowledged as his grandfather's heir, a position which he forfeited in 1324, on the birth of the future David II. Forty-seven years later, when

David against all expectation had failed to perpetuate his dynasty, Robert II was crowned and anointed at Scone, on 26 March 1371.

Perhaps a man advanced to supreme power by the delayed action of chance could not have been expected to be a very decisive ruler; but it was unfortunate that by the standards of his time he was well past his prime, and in poor health, so that he lacked the energy required of a king who was responsible for every aspect of government.

Robert II's only personal achievement was an abundant provision for the succession, for he had fathered at least twenty-one children, thirteen of whom were born in wedlock. However, he had been twice married, and to his first wife, Elizabeth Mure of Rowallan, he had been related within the 'forbidden degrees' of kinship. Yet for some years he had neglected to obtain the necessary Papal dispensation for their marriage. In consequence, their elder children were technically illegitimate, and it was questionable whether the tardily obtained dispensation served to legitimize them retrospectively. The children of Robert II's second marriage, to Euphemia of Ross, were indisputably legitimate, and the resultant feud between the descendants of the two marriages continued for generations and culminated in murder.

Robert II upheld the efficacy of the dispensation, and insisted that the succession should be settled upon his eldest son, John, Earl of Carrick, and his heirs, and if this line should fail, upon his second son Robert, Earl of Fife, and his heirs, then upon his third son Alexander, Lord of Badenoch, and his heirs. Only if these three lines should fail was the succession to pass, on the same terms, to the King's sons by his second marriage, David, Earl of Strathearn, and Walter, Earl of Atholl, and their heirs. This arrangement, known as a *tailzie*, was confirmed by an Act of Parliament of 1373.

In 1377, after the death of Edward III, who had grown peaceable in senility, war broke out again between Scotland and England, as a side issue of the Hundred Years' War between England and France. In effect it was 'a war of chivalry on the Borders', and King Robert II was a mere spectator of the hostilities. He had already delegated his authority to John of Carrick, who proved a scarcely more vigorous ruler. In 1388 Carrick was kicked by a horse and he received an injury which left him lame for life. When Robert II died on 19 April 1390 he was succeeded by a semi-invalid who was already over fifty.

Carrick took the name of Robert III, because John appeared to have been an unlucky name for kings: John of England had been obliged to acknowledge England as a fief of the Papacy; John Balliol of Scotland had been the vassal of Edward I; and John II of France had been captured by the English at Poitiers. Robert III's subjects used his new style only officially, and called him 'John Faranyeir' – i.e., John of Yesteryear. It has often been remarked that the change of name did not alter the omens.

Between Robert III's accession and his coronation occurred one of the most notorious outrages ever committed against the royal authority. On 17 June 1390 the King's brother, Alexander (who while serving as Justiciar of the North had so much abused his authority as to win himself the name of 'the Wolf of Badenoch'), in pursuit of a feud with the Bishop of Moray, burned the Cathedral and the town of Elgin, the parish church and the Maison Dieu hospital. The noble shell of the Cathedral still remains, as a memorial to the splendour which thirteenth-century Scotland had been capable of raising to the glory of God, and as a witness to the disorder into which the kingdom had fallen. The Wolf of Badenoch and the 'wyld wykked Hielandmen' who had abetted him went unpunished because the central government had lost the power to impose order.

The disorder in the Highlands continued unchecked as the reign progressed. In September 1396 an attempt was made to put an end to a feud between the Clans Chattan and Kay by organizing a trial by battle on the North Inch of Perth, in the presence of Robert III and his court. Thirty champions from each clan met in mortal combat, and when only twelve men survived, the King put an end to the fighting by casting down his baton. Though the survivors may have been glad enough to obey the regal gesture, the so-called 'Battle of the Clans' does not appear to have had any long-term effect in pacifying the Highlands.

Robert III acknowledged his incapacity by delegating his authority to his next brother, Robert, Earl of Fife, who possessed both ability and ambition. But by abdicating his responsibility, though not his Crown, Robert III permitted a power struggle to develop within his family. By his Queen, Annabella Drummond, Robert III had two sons, David and James. For his heir, David, and his brother, the Earl of Fife, Robert III created Scotland's first dukedoms, of Rothesay and Albany respectively. In 1399 David of Rothesay acted as Lieutenant of the Kingdom; but he lived wildly and governed incompetently, and in 1401 Albany persuaded the King to order his arrest.

Albany was permitted to take Rothesay into his own custody, in which he died the following year. There were rumours that Rothesay had been starved to death, and Albany was obliged to face a judicial inquiry, which predictably exonerated him.

Probably Robert III continued to suspect his brother of murder, for he decided to send his surviving son for safety to the French court. In March 1406 the eleven-year-old Prince James put to sea, only to be captured by English pirates, who took him to the court of Henry IV. He remained a prisoner for eighteen years. On 4 April 1406 Robert III, 'powerless and decrepit', died shortly after receiving the news of his son's capture. The Scottish Parliament at once acknowledged the captive James as King of Scots, but Albany became Governor of Scotland, and for the next fourteen years he ruled as king in all but name. Though personally he inspired more awe than Robert II or Robert III, he too failed to impose order on the kingdom.

The most unhappy consequence of the ineffectual government of the early Stewarts was a renewed dichotomy between the Highlands and the Lowlands. It was from this time onwards that the Gaelic speech of the Highlands and the Scots speech of the Lowlands exerted a divisive influence, making the two halves of Scotland seem foreign and inimical to each other.

In the Highlands, the feudalism which had advanced under the later kings of the House of Dunkeld decayed, and from the late fourteenth century the clan system became increasingly organized. Clansmen were bound together by a notional kinship, the belief in their descent from a common ancestor, and the essentially paternalistic authority of their chief is

St Margaret of
Scotland, wife of
Malcolm III, as
depicted in a
fifteenth-century
Book of Hours.

King David II, after
his capture at the
battle of Neville's
Cross, is received by
Edward III of
England (from a
fourteenth-century
manuscript).

A silver groat of James III, a fine coin which is thought to bear the earliest Renaissance coin-portrait produced in northern Europe.

A striking profile of James V on a gold coin known as 'the bonnet piece'.

A contemporary drawing of James IV, by Jacques le Boucq

Mary, Queen of Scots, The Morton Portrait; artist unknown

James VI and I, artist unknown

Medal of Charles I, by Nicholas Briot

Charles II as a boy, by William Dobson

perfectly illustrated by the single word 'clan', which is simply the Gaelic *clann*, meaning children. In the Lowlands there was a parallel development in the power of the 'name' or 'kin' to bind men together as followers of the head of their family: Hamiltons, Douglases, Homes, Hepburns, Livingstones and other great families formed the Lowland equivalents of the Highland clans. The difference was principally created by the economic differences between the two parts of the kingdom. In the Lowlands trade and agriculture continued despite internal disorder and foreign war; peaceful and ordered existence was the desire if not the achievement of Lowland society. Highland society remained pastoral and heroic. Agriculture was discouraged by the poor quality of the land, and the wealth of the clans was in their cattle. The clansmen were cattle raisers – and frequently cattle rustlers – and warriors. While the 'kin' contained men of diverse professions who were expected to offer the head of their name political support, the clan had an essentially warlike character, and provided its chief with his personal army.

The threat of the clans to the central government was embodied in the early fifteenth century in the rise of the semi-autonomous Lordship of the Isles, under the chiefs of the Clan MacDonald. Great terror was caused in the Lowlands in 1411 when Donald, Lord of the Isles, claimed the earldom of Ross in right of his wife, seized Inverness, and marched on Aberdeen with an army of Highlanders and Islesmen. He was defeated at the Battle of Harlaw by Alexander Stewart, Earl of Mar, son of the Wolf of Badenoch, supported by the Provost and Burgesses of Aberdeen. The battle was long remembered as 'the Red Harlaw' and popularly imagined to have been a battle between the Highlands and the Lowlands. In reality, Donald's aims had been personal, and his defeat illustrated that his power was not equal even to his limited ambitions. But the government was not strong enough to follow up the victory of Harlaw. The Lordship of the Isles survived to be a thorn in the flesh of successive kings, and the Highlands remained beyond the Governor Albany's control.

Albany was naturally preoccupied by Anglo-Scottish hostilities. His son, Murdoch Stewart, had been captured by the English at the Battle of Homildon Hill in 1402, and he remained a prisoner until 1416. When his ransom was negotiated, no attempt was made to liberate the young King James, which suggested that Albany hoped to transfer the Crown to his own family. He died in 1420, over eighty years old, and Murdoch succeeded him as Governor. Had he been able and ambitious he might have become King, but his government foundered after four years of mismanagement. In 1424 King James I returned to a kingdom which welcomed him as much as it needed him.

That the House of Stewart had survived its unimpressive beginnings illustrated the strength of the Scottish monarchy as an institution. The monarchy was honoured when the King was not, because it personified the identity of the nation. Its theoretical powers remained unimpaired, and in the hands of a strong king it could give the nation security and strength. The prestige of the Stewart dynasty began with the reign of James I.

During his years in England James had not always been kept a close prisoner; sometimes he had been permitted to take part in the life of the court. To the credit of Henry IV, his education had not been neglected. He became a man of many talents: athlete, linguist, musician, singer and poet. In 1423, the last year of his captivity, occurred the romantic episode which James narrated in his poem *The Kingis Quair* (i.e., *The King's Book*). James was probably imprisoned at Windsor when he looked out of his window early one morning and saw a beautiful young woman walking in the garden below. As he described the moment in his poem:

> ... therewith kest I doune myne eye ageyne
> Quare as I saw, walking under the toure,
> Full secretly now cummin hir to pleyne,
> The fairest or the freschest younge floure
> That evir I saw, me thoght, before that houre...

The woman with whom he fell in love at first sight was Lady Joan Beaufort, a great-granddaughter of Edward III. Love and policy worked in rare accord, for the Beauforts were as eager to see Lady Joan become Queen of Scotland as the Scots were to regain their King. Thenceforward negotiations for James's release progressed rapidly. On 2 February 1424 James married Lady Joan Beaufort in the church which is now Southwark Cathedral, and they journeyed together to Scotland in the spring.

James was appalled by his first impression of the disorder of his kingdom. 'If God grant me life and aid,' he is reported to have said, 'even the life of a dog, throughout all the realm I will make the key keep the castle and the bracken bush the cow.' His anger turned naturally against the family of the Governor who had left him in captivity. The old Duke of Albany was fortunate to have died, for as soon as the King's power was firmly established Duke Murdoch was executed, together with his father-in-law and his sons.

James I made it clear that he preferred to be feared than loved, yet a modern historian has written of him '. . . none of James's predecessors or successors was so committed as he was, persistently, determinedly and emotionally, to pursuing the common weal.' The first legislation of a king who was remembered above all as a lawgiver aimed at providing 'firm and secure peace' throughout his kingdom, and the purpose of many ensuing enactments was the punishment of rebels and violent criminals, the prevention of crime and the protection of the helpless mass of the population which had suffered so much during the preceding half-century of disorder.

The King sought to improve the quality of both criminal and civil justice. In 1426 he founded a new court, known simply as 'the Session', which consisted of the Chancellor and 'certain discreet persons of the three Estates', to hear cases which previously had been brought before the King and Council, or before Parliament. James's concern that justice should be available to the poorest of his subjects was shown by his appointment of a 'poor man's advocate'.

James I had less success in extending the rule of law to the Highlands, though this was not for lack of trying. In 1428 he invited fifty Highland chiefs to a gathering at Inverness, and had them seized and imprisoned. A few were executed as a warning to the rest, while the others were held captive in various royal castles. Among those who fell into the King's trap was Alexander, Lord of the Isles, son of the protagonist of

Harlaw. For a time he was imprisoned at Perth, but he escaped, and burned the burgh of Inverness, in revenge for his wrongs. Defeated in Lochaber by the royal forces, he was captured and imprisoned again, and obliged to make a humiliating act of submission to the King, and to stand before the high altar of Holyrood Abbey dressed as a penitent. While the Lord of the Isles remained in prison during 1431, some of his kinsmen defeated what was intended to be a peace-keeping force, commanded by Alexander Stewart, Earl of Mar, in a skirmish near Inverlochy. Thereafter, James I changed his policy, and released the Lord of the Isles, possibly on condition of his making no further trouble, for he kept the peace for the remainder of the reign.

In an attempt to heal the breach between Highlands and Lowlands James I frequently held his court at Perth, which he made the nearest approximation to a capital which was possible while government was still peripatetic. Had Perth become the capital of Scotland the unity of the kingdom might have been restored; but as the century progressed the influence of Anglo-Scottish relations drew the centre of government to Edinburgh, ill-placed for administering the remote north-west.

At Perth James met his death on 21 February 1437, the victim of the feud which had resulted from Robert II's two marriages. The purpose of the conspiracy against him was to win the Crown for Walter, Earl of Atholl, the surviving son of Robert II and Euphemia of Ross, and the succession for his grandson. The King was staying in the Dominican Priory at Perth, which was not defensible. Late at night the conspirators forced an entry and stabbed James to death in a vault beneath his bedchamber, where the Queen attempted to hide him. It was a savage end for a man who had been a constant enemy of violent crime, and a mismanaged plot which killed the King and spared his six-year-old son. If the conspirators had expected a spontaneous rising in Atholl's favour they had miscalculated. The nobility of Scotland accepted the established royal line, and the commons mourned a King who had made Scotland fit to live in. The Edinburgh populace shouted its approval of his murderers' death by torture, culminating in the coronation of Atholl with a crown of red-hot iron.

The child King James II was crowned in the Abbey of Holyrood, breaking the long tradition of coronation at Scone. He must have been a pathetic little figure in the midst of all the splendour, for half his face was covered by a purple birth-mark. The fame of his disfigurement led him to be mentioned in François Villon's *Ballade des Seigneurs de Temps Jadis* as

> ... Le Roy Scotiste
> Qui demy face ot, ce dit-on,
> Vermeille comme une amatiste
> Depuis le front jusqu'au menton.

James II's succession was uncontested, but his minority was troubled by the conflicts of men who strove to control him. The fifth Earl of Douglas, whose mother was a daughter of Robert III, was appointed Governor of Scotland, but he failed to control the ambitions of Sir William Crichton and Sir Alexander Livingstone, the keepers of Edinburgh Castle and Stirling Castle respectively, each of whom gained power in turn by seizing the young King. After the death of the Governor in 1439, Crichton and Living-stone united to destroy his ambitious son, William, sixth Earl of Douglas. On 24 November 1440 the young Earl and his brother were entertained in Edinburgh Castle at the notorious 'Black Dinner', at which they were treacherously seized and beheaded before the eyes of the King. It was widely believed that the seventh Earl of Douglas, James 'the Gross', who was great-uncle to the murdered youths, had been accessory to the crime. Thereafter he and the Living-stones amassed increasing power at Crichton's ex-pense, and for the rest of the minority dominated Scotland.

James II asserted his authority at the age of nineteen in 1449, when a prestigious marriage to Mary of Guelders, niece of Philip 'the Good', Duke of Bur-gundy, may have helped him to overthrow the Livingstones. The Douglases presented a greater problem. William, eighth Earl of Douglas, son of James the Gross, married his cousin, 'the Fair Maid of Galloway', sister of the earl who had been murdered at the Black Dinner. A vast accretion of estates, stretching from Galloway across the Borders, made him the greatest magnate of southern Scotland. James II had no wish to see a Lowland equivalent of the Lordship of the Isles develop, and he determined to destroy the Douglas power.

The crisis of the King's relations with the House of Douglas came in 1452, when he discovered that the Earl was creating a network of alliances with England, the Lord of the Isles, and the Earl of Crawford. James summoned Douglas to Stirling, revealed his knowl-edge of this traitorous diplomacy, and demanded that Douglas repudiate his allies and reaffirm his allegiance.

Douglas refused, and in the ensuing quarrel James stabbed him to death. The Earl's next brother, who inherited his title and married his widow, attempted to continue his resistance to the Crown; but the Douglas power was broken at the Battle of Arkinholm in 1455, after which the ninth Earl fled to England, and his estates were forfeited. He survived to become a pensioner of England, and an increasingly futile troublemaker in the next reign.

It has been a commonplace of Scottish history that the fifteenth century witnessed a conflict between the Crown and the nobility, which the struggle between James II and the House of Douglas appears to exemplify. In fact, it exemplifies the very opposite. If the Crown had not enjoyed the support of a majority of the nobles, it would not have possessed the power to ruin a family which had grown so great. James II made it clear that he did not fear a powerful nobility, for he did not hesitate to aggrandize men who had shown him loyalty. Indeed, he deliberately enhanced the power of certain families to assist the government in controlling their localities. The earldom of Huntly, which gave the Gordons pre-eminence in the north-east, and the earldom of Argyll, which established the power of the Campbells, both date from his reign.

James II's success in re-establishing the rule of law won him the congratulations of the Parliament of 1458, which also entreated him to continue his good work, 'that God may be empleased of him, and all his lieges may pray for him to God, and give thanks to Him that sends them such a Prince to be their governor and defender'.

Scotland had reason to feel gratitude to James II, for his strong rule contrasted with the disorder which had broken out in England between the Royal Houses of York and Lancaster. In the early stages of the Wars of the Roses, Yorkist patronage of the fugitive Earl of Douglas gave James II an excuse to intervene, ostensibly as the ally of the Lancastrian King Henry VI. James's desire was to recapture Roxburgh Castle, which had been in English hands since the reign of David II. The fact that it was held by a Yorkist governor provided the pretext for the Scottish attack. James II was an enthusiast for the developing military science of gunnery. His great cannon, which had been used with devastating effect against the Douglas strongholds, were dragged to Roxburgh and positioned on the flat ground by the River Tweed, beside Kelso. On 3 August 1460 James was supervising the bombardment, standing close to one of the guns, which had been overcharged with gunpowder. The gun burst with the force of the explosion, and the King was instantaneously killed.

In the face of this tragedy the widowed Queen showed courage and resource. She brought her eldest son James to Roxburgh and exhorted the Scots to continue the siege. Within a few days the castle surrendered, and the fortifications were razed to prevent its future occupation. The new reign began with the good omen of victory when the eight-year-old James III was crowned on 10 August in Kelso Abbey. But unhappily Scotland was faced with another royal minority, which proved to be only the second of a series. The evil consequence of these minorities was that they caused a lack of continuity in effective rule. Successive kings had to expend their energies, and sometimes give their lives, to creating the normality and order which they ought to have inherited. The remarkable aspect of the recurrent situation, illustrative of the Scottish respect for monarchy, was that though the young kings were manipulated by ambitious men no attempt was made to wrest the crown from the Stewart dynasty even when it appeared defenceless.

At the beginning of James III's minority the principal authority was exercised by the Queen Mother, and after her death in 1463 by Bishop Kennedy of St Andrews. Fortunately Kennedy lived long enough to save Scotland from the dangerous activities of the exiled Earl of Douglas and the Lord of the Isles, who made a treaty with Edward IV, the victorious Yorkist King of England, whereby Scotland was to be partitioned between the traitors, who were to rule as vassals of England. Kennedy, by abandoning the Lancastrian alliance, and making a long-term truce with Edward IV, eliminated the potential threat.

After the death of Bishop Kennedy in 1465 the pattern of James III's minority resembled that of his father. In 1466 James was kidnapped by Lord Boyd of Kilmarnock and his brother Sir Alexander Boyd, who was the King's military tutor and the keeper of Edinburgh Castle. For the remainder of the minority the Boyds ruled Scotland in the King's name, and sought to secure their power by the marriage of Lord Boyd's son to the King's sister Mary, a *mésalliance* which James resented. However, Lord Boyd showed himself an able diplomatist, especially in negotiating the King's marriage. In 1469 James married Margaret of Denmark, daughter of Christian I of Denmark, Norway and Sweden. The estates of the Norwegian Crown in Orkney and Shetland were pledged against the payment of her dowry, and as her father failed to raise the agreed sum the pledge was forfeited. The Boyds were overthrown by James III at the time of his marriage, but he completed Lord Boyd's policy by formally annexing the Northern Isles in 1472, thus bringing the territories of the Crown of Scots to their greatest extent.

The character of James III has been the subject of controversy. Sixteenth-century and later historians represented him as a weak king addicted to lowborn favourites, and as a man whose artistic tastes and lack of martial prowess cost him the respect of the warlike nobility. Recent research has shown this thumbnail sketch to be over-simplified. James III could act with energy, as he showed in the overthrow of the Boyds, and at other crises of the reign; and though he seems to have lacked enthusiasm for the routine of administration, he was an astute diplomatist. His artistic tastes led him to collect a circle of intellectual 'familiars' (as he himself described them); but they were not the 'lowborn favourites' that later generations imagined. The root of James III's unpopularity was probably that while he was a less accessible king than either his father or his grandfather, he aspired to a more absolute authority than they had possessed. At the same time, he lacked the force of personality to equal either of them, and the tact which might have achieved his purpose by other means.

James III was unfortunate in having two popular younger brothers, Alexander, Duke of Albany and John, Earl of Mar. In 1479 both were arrested upon suspicion of treasonable activities. Mar died in prison, but Albany escaped, to pursue ambitions which fully justified the King's suspicion. Albany went first to France, where King Louis XI gave him an aristocratic bride, but refused him military aid; he then crossed to England, where he found a more active patron in Edward IV. Anglo-Scottish relations had again deteriorated, and Edward IV was tempted to revive the aspirations of the early Plantagenets. On 10 August 1482 he proclaimed Albany 'Alexander IV' of Scotland, and sent him north with an army commanded by Richard, Duke of Gloucester (the future Richard III) to establish him as a vassal king.

The Scottish response was predictable, yet the outcome was unforeseen. James III mustered an army to combat the English threat, but at Lauder, on the route south, a group of noblemen led by the Earl of Angus (a 'Red' Douglas, related to the ruined branch of the family, which was known as the 'Black') rebelled against the King and hanged a group of the King's familiars over the Bridge of Lauder. The King was then forcibly taken back to Edinburgh and confined in the Castle. But the revolt was a palace revolution, not a threat to the Crown. It proved not even to be an attempt to overthrow the King, for when Albany arrived he found himself unacceptable as a substitute for his brother. The sovereign, though personally unpopular, still seemed preferable to a king who sought to install himself with English patronage. Albany was obliged to compose his differences with James III, and Richard of Gloucester contented himself with the capture of Berwick-on-Tweed, which has remained in English hands ever since.

Albany, however, was a compulsive traitor, and upon the discovery of his renewed intrigues with England, he fled south in 1484. By this time the hard-pressed Richard III could spare him no support, but he found a down-and-out ally in the Earl of

Douglas. Their joint invasion of Scotland was defeated by local resistance at Lochmaben, near Dumfries. Douglas was captured and condemned by James III's merciful justice to monastic life at the Abbey of Lindores. Albany escaped, and fled to France, where he was killed at a tournament the following year.

James III's difficulties appeared to be at an end. After Richard III's death at Bosworth in 1485, James made peace with his supplanter Henry VII, the first Tudor King of England. But the peace with England was itself unpopular, and when James would have been wise to seek support, he showed himself as tactless and self-willed as he had been in youth.

When the King's eldest son, Prince James, was fifteen, he was manipulated by a resurgent opposition, again led by the Earl of Angus. Faced by rebellion James III still drew strong support, including contingents from the Highlands. But the rebels defeated the royal army at the Battle of Sauchieburn, near Stirling, and clinched their victory by murdering the King after his flight from the battlefield. James III, whose reputation has never stood high, deserves more credit than he has received. Until the last rebellion, he successfully defended Scotland against English ambitions and internal treasons. He sought peace, patronized the arts, and retained his throne while that of England was occupied by Henry VI, Edward IV, Edward V, Richard III and usurped by Henry VII.

King James IV, who matured early and rapidly asserted his authority, suffered agonies of conscience for his father's murder. As a self-imposed penance he wore an iron chain round his waist for the rest of his life, and added links to it as the years passed, so that time and habit should never be allowed to lighten the burden. Despite his slightly morbid piety, which was characteristic of his generation, James was a man of great intellectual energy. He spoke eight languages, including Gaelic, which was remarked upon by the Spanish Ambassador, Pedro de Ayala, who called it 'the language of the savages who live in some parts of Scotland . . .' This comment may be the measure of the dichotomy of Scotland by the end of the fifteenth century. James IV was aware of the necessity to re-unify the kingdom, but as with his predecessors, much of his attention was preoccupied by foreign politics.

During the early years of James IV's reign relations with England were uneasy, for James supported the Yorkist pretender Perkin Warbeck, probably in retaliation for English support of Albany. Henry VII, however, had no wish to fight the Scots. His chief desire was to secure his dynasty, so he offered an alliance and proposed a marriage between James IV and his eldest daughter, Margaret Tudor. The marriage took place in 1503 when James was thirty and Margaret was thirteen. Of their six children, one son, born in 1512, survived to reign as James V; but their marriage led ultimately to the Union of Crowns, when their great-grandson James VI became James I of England in 1603. One hundred years earlier, however, James IV saw a greater likelihood of Scotland's becoming an English satellite. With the hope of securing the independence of Scotland, when he signed a peace treaty with England he refused to repudiate the auld alliance with France.

While James appeared to be prudently hedging his bets, his policy could be maintained only so long as England and France were at peace. But he hoped that

European peace could be maintained by a grand
design. In 1453 Constantinople had fallen to the
Turks, and the ensuing half-century had witnessed the
advance of Turkish power in Eastern Europe and the
Mediterranean. A new crusade to hold back the Turks
and to unite the rulers of Western Europe was a scheme
in which James IV showed more vision than his
contemporaries.

During the early years of the sixteenth century the
rulers whom James IV had hoped to see united pursued
ambitions which led them into war. In 1508, Pope
Julius II, ambitious to increase the secular power of the
Papacy, formed the League of Cambrai with France
against the power of the Venetian Republic. But,
having lost control of the hostilities which he had
initiated, in 1511 Julius negotiated the mis-named
Holy League, to expel the French from Italy. The
Papacy, Spain, Venice, England and the Holy Roman
Empire allied against France, and James IV faced the
consequences of his adherence to the auld alliance
when King Louis XII appealed for support to his only
ally, the King of Scots.

Henry VIII of England, who had succeeded in 1509,
had treated his brother-in-law James IV in an arrogant
and bellicose manner since the beginning of the reign.
The consequent deterioration of Anglo-Scottish relations decided James in favour of France. When Henry
VIII invaded France in 1513 James sent him an
ultimatum. Henry's reply, that he was 'the very
owner' of Scotland, and that when he returned from
France he would 'expulse' James from his kingdom
clearly showed that if France were defeated the
independence of Scotland would be in danger again.
The reality of the situation demolishes the myth that

James IV went to war on behalf of France from mistaken motives of chivalry.

At the end of August 1513 James invaded England, to be met by an army commanded by the Earl of Surrey, who ten years previously had escorted Margaret Tudor to her wedding. On 9 September James IV and a great host of his subjects, prominent and obscure, met their deaths on the 'carnage pile' of Flodden Field. The defeat seemed a tragedy of unexampled magnitude because it cost Scotland the life of a well-loved king, and of many noblemen and many churchmen (including the young Archbishop of St Andrews, who was the King's illegitimate son). The rank and file of the army comprised a cross-section of the nation: Highlanders and Islesmen, Lowlanders and Borderers (the Borderers were the 'Flowers of the Forest' later lamented by romantic poets).

Yet, despite the extravagant lamentation it inspired, the battle had no decisive results. James IV's seventeen-month-old son succeeded, and a regency government was set up; England and France made a peace in which Scotland was included. The transformation of Scotland which occurred during the sixteenth century was unconnected with temporal warfare.

CHAPTER FIVE

The Transformation of Scotland
1513 – 1603

During the reigns of James III, James IV and James V there was a continuity in Scottish culture which the Battle of Flodden did not interrupt.

The flowering of the Scottish Renaissance is usually ascribed to the reign of James IV, but its beginning belongs to that of his father. James III patronized the arts with informed taste. He commissioned an altarpiece from the Flemish artist, Hugo van der Goes, surviving panels of which bear portraits of James and his Queen. In the later years of his reign he issued a beautiful coinage on which the King's head is thought to be the first renaissance coin portrait produced in northern Europe. In boyhood his tutor was a humanist scholar named Archibald Whitelaw, who subsequently became his secretary. The influence of Whitelaw perhaps may be discerned in the broad education provided for the future James IV. While James IV's interests were less specifically aesthetic than his father's he actively encouraged every aspect of intellectual life. He was associated with Bishop William Elphinstone in founding King's College, Aberdeen, in 1495; he granted a charter to the Royal College of Surgeons of Edinburgh in 1506; and he encouraged the establishment of Scotland's first printing press in 1508.

The reigns of James III, and his son and grandson,

witnessed the first great period of Scottish poetry, in the work of the 'makars', courtly poets in whose poetry highly wrought craftsmanship and intense lyricism were finely blended. Robert Henryson (c.1430–1500) wrote his *Testament of Cresseid* for a court audience in the reign of James III, and William Dunbar (c.1460–1514) produced the greater part of his work in that of James IV. He celebrated the marriage of James IV and Margaret Tudor in *The Thrissill and the Rois*, and in the *Lament for the Makaris* he names many poets whose works are no longer known.

Religious poetry, richly ornamented and profoundly pious, was written by Dunbar and many of these contemporaries and predecessors. A beautiful example is Dunbar's *Of the Nativitie of Christ*:

> *Rorate celi desuper!**
> Hevins distil your balmy shouris,
> For now is risen the bricht day ster
> Fro the rose Mary, flour of flouris.
> The clear Son, whom no cloud devouris,
> Surminting Phebus in the est
> Is cumin of his hevinly touris;
> *Et nobis puer natus est.*†

Yet Dunbar and his contemporaries, who could write with such devotion, also displayed a vein of anti-clericalism in their satirical verse.

Gavin Douglas (c.1474–1522), a son of the fifth Earl of Angus, and Bishop of Dunkeld, extended the range of the Scots vernacular in a superb translation of

---

*The second line paraphrases the first.
†'And unto us a child is born'

Virgil's *Aeneid* into Scots verse, adding an original prologue to each book. Douglas's *Eneados* was written in 1512–13, but was not published until 1553.

The greatest courtly poet of the next reign was Sir David Lindsay of the Mount (c. 1486–1555) who was Master Usher to the young James V, and later Lyon King of Arms. Though not so fine a literary craftsman as Henryson, Dunbar or Douglas, Lindsay was an eloquent poet and a pungent satirist, whose works reached a wider audience than those of his predecessors. The prolific Lindsay's most popular work was *The Satire of the Three Estates*, a satirical drama which castigated the shortcomings of Church, State and Society. Its long performances (in 1540, 1552 and 1554) were appreciated by Lindsay's contemporaries, and an abridged version has been revived in recent years.

The increasing anti-clericalism in the writings of the poets points to the central weakness which led to the transformation of Scotland in the sixteenth century: the lamentable condition of the Church. The Universal Church of the Middle Ages had become less Catholic and more national as a result of the Great Schism – the period between 1378 and 1417 during which rival popes had competed for the allegiance of Christian kingdoms. With the decline of spiritual authority different countries had developed different national abuses. In Scotland the ultimately destructive flaw in the Church was the increasingly secular character of the higher clergy.

In 1487 James III obtained from Pope Innocent VIII the concession that his nominations to bishoprics and abbacies would be considered at the Court of Rome. This small loophole soon let in a flood of unsuitable appointments. In 1504 James IV obtained the primatial see for his eleven-year-old illegitimate son, Alexander. The boy Archbishop was a brilliant pupil of Erasmus, and he might have become an outstanding ecclesiastic had he not been killed at Flodden when he was twenty. Nonetheless, his extreme youth was inappropriate to the primacy of Scotland.

The royal example was followed by noble families, which secured bishoprics and benefices for younger sons, most of whom did not have genuine vocations. In consequence, dioceses and monasteries lacked spiritual leadership and discipline. The wealth of the Church was creamed off by its dignitaries, leaving the parish clergy miserably underpaid, and as a result good recruits to the priesthood were few. Impoverished, ignorant and often immoral parish priests could neither nourish the spiritual lives of the people nor keep their respect. The situation grew worse as the reign of James V progressed, and so the seed-bed of the Reformation was well prepared.

James V, so far the youngest of his dynasty to succeed, had a characteristically troubled childhood. Under the will of James IV, Margaret Tudor was appointed guardian of her son, which made her unofficially head of state, but her authority was unacceptable, since she was known to be devoted to her brother Henry VIII, whose intentions towards Scotland had been made clear before Flodden. Anti-English feeling led the surviving leaders of the nobility to turn to the auld alliance. They requested the Franco-Scottish John Stuart, Duke of Albany, the son of James III's traitorous brother, to come to Scotland and assume the governorship. He accepted, and between 1515 and 1524, during three periods of residence in Scotland, he provided an isolated example of political honesty among the power struggles surrounding the throne. His most useful achievement was to negotiate the Treaty of Rouen in 1521, whereby James V was to marry a daughter of Francis I of France.

Albany was opposed by Queen Margaret, who aspired to rule and would have done so according to the dictates of Henry VIII. In the hope of gaining a pro-English supporter, Margaret married Archibald Douglas, sixth Earl of Angus. The Earl was anglophile, but his ambition was to win power for himself, not to share it with Margaret. Their political and domestic strife was a great assistance to Albany. After 1524 Francis I required Albany's services in the Italian Wars, and Angus gained power in Scotland by a *coup d'état* at the end of 1525. Although the young James V was declared of age to rule in 1526, he remained in effect his stepfather's prisoner until 1528. Queen Margaret obtained an annulment of her marriage to Angus, and married a third husband, Henry Stewart, Lord Methven. As a result she forfeited all hope of regaining power, and for a time lost contact with her son.

The Earl of Angus culpably neglected his stepson's education, and was believed to have arranged an early sexual initiation for him, in the hope that precocious debauchery would deflect him from interest in government. Fortunately this irresponsible policy failed. Though James V was poorly educated by comparison with most renaissance princes, he showed natural artistic taste; and though the pursuit of women remained his chief pleasure all his life, he was just as determined as his predecessors to escape from tutelage and rule his kingdom.

In 1528 James escaped from Angus's custody, and forced his stepfather, and many of the 'name' of Douglas, to flee to England. The ruthlessness of James's character soon led him to be feared by many of his influential subjects. 'So sore a dread King, and so ill-beloved of his subjects,' wrote a contemporary, 'was never in this land.' However, he was popular with the commons, who benefited from his hereditary dedication to law and order, and appreciated another aspect of his character, which was a penchant for disguise, in search of low life and amorous adventure.

In 1529 and 1530 James V used rough justice to discipline the Highlands and the Borders, where disorder had once more broken out during the minority. Thereafter quiet ensued throughout most of the reign, until a rebellion occurred in 1539, led by a chief named Donald Gorm of Sleat, who claimed the Lordship of the Isles, which had been suppressed by James IV. Donald Gorm was defeated and killed, but his rebellion determined James V to assert the royal authority in the remotest areas of the north-west by a circumnavigation of the kingdom. In 1540 he visited Orkney, rounded Cape Wrath, landed on many of the Western Isles, and concluded his voyage at Dumbarton, bringing back many hostages to ensure the good behaviour of the Highland and Island chiefs. After his return, Parliament enacted the annexation of the Lordship of the Isles to the Crown: 'Lord of the Isles' remains to the present day one of the titles of the heir to the throne.

In his foreign policy James V firmly adhered to the

auld alliance, chiefly as a bulwark against the power of Henry VIII, with whom his relations had been uneasy from the beginning of his personal rule. In the autumn of 1536 James visited France, and on 1 January 1537, in accordance with the Treaty of Rouen, he married Madeleine, daughter of Francis I. Madeleine's delicate health had made her father reluctant to allow the marriage, and his fears proved justified, for she died in July, shortly after reaching Scotland. However, Francis clearly bore James no ill-will, for the next year he gave him a second French bride, the beautiful and intelligent Mary of Guise, whom he created an honorary Daughter of France, to raise her from ducal to regal status. She bore James V two sons, who died in infancy, and in 1542 she gave birth to a daughter, who survived to reign as Mary, Queen of Scots.

The generous dowries which James received with his two French brides enabled him to indulge his taste for building, and express the inspiration which he had derived from his visits to French *châteaux*. Between 1537 and 1540 he metamorphosed some of the royal castles into renaissance palaces. Falkland Palace, and the Palace Building in Stirling Castle, are monuments to his taste and his political affiliations.

Alliance with a great Catholic power, and personal conviction, both inclined James V to orthodoxy at a period when Reformation doctrines were making rapid headway in Europe. As early as 1525 the Scottish Parliament passed Acts against the importation of Lutheran literature, and Henry VIII's encouragement of the Reformation for personal reasons, culminating in his declaration of his own supremacy over the English Church in 1534, only served to confirm James's determination to take the opposite path.

Having chosen Catholicism, James made the Papacy pay dearly for his orthodoxy. With the Pope's agreement he imposed a tax of £10,000 per annum on the Scottish prelates, on the pretext of endowing a 'College of Justice' or body of salaried judges in Scotland. But though the College of Justice was indeed founded, largely from the membership of the existing 'Session', most of the aptly-named 'Great Tax' went into the coffers of the King. Furthermore, five of James's numerous bastards were made 'commendators' or lay abbots of Scotland's richest abbeys, thus further weakening the Church on which the King had chosen to stake the religious future of his kingdom. James V expected the Church to conduct its own necessary reform, but he did not provide it with either the example or the means to do so.

James V's years of achievement were followed by a sudden *débâcle*. In 1541 a configuration of international alliances, in which James V was aligned with Francis I, and Henry VIII with his enemy the Emperor Charles V, echoed the situation of 1513. But the Reformation complicated the issue. James V was the ally of the Papacy, but in the course of his reign many of his nobility had converted to Protestantism, and they were unwilling to fight for an ill-beloved king against their English co-religionists. In the autumn of 1542 Henry VIII, renewing his claim to overlordship of Scotland, sent an invading army against his nephew, and James's force, commanded by his unpopular favourite, Oliver Sinclair, was defeated at the Battle of Solway Moss, on 24 November.

James, who had been taken ill before the invasion, received the news of the disaster, closely followed by that of the birth of his daughter. He doubted that the independence of the kingdom could survive the double blow, or that the Crown could remain in his dynasty. Dying, of an unspecified illness aggravated by despair, he prophesied 'It cam' wi' a lass, it will pass wi' a lass.' He imagined that the Crown which had come to the Stewarts through Margery Bruce would be lost by his defenceless daughter, who was one week old when he died on 14 December. In fact it was lost on the death of another 'lass', his descendant Queen Anne.

As before, the Scots showed themselves stalwart in defeat, and loyal to the Crown. They acknowledged their infant Queen, and appointed a regency. The Governor for Mary, Queen of Scots, was James Hamilton, second Earl of Arran, a great-grandson of King James II. He favoured the Protestant and English interest, and in 1543 he signed a treaty with Henry VIII, by which Mary was to marry Henry's son, the future Edward VI.

The Queen-Dowager, Mary of Guise, and her astute adviser Cardinal Beaton, Archbishop of St Andrews, who had been temporarily eclipsed after the death of James V, swiftly reasserted themselves, and repudiated the treaty before the end of the year. Henry VIII retaliated with two invasions, in 1544 and 1545, a policy ill-calculated to win Scottish support. Indeed, the atrocities and devastations committed by his forces were dourly nicknamed 'the Rough Wooing'. Henry pressed his policy to the point of encouraging the murder of Cardinal Beaton in 1546, but when Henry himself died the following year Scotland was as far as ever from becoming a satellite of England. The Regent for the boy King Edward VI led an invasion in 1547, and defeated the Scots at the Battle of Pinkie Cleugh. Mary of Guise and her supporters then appealed to

France for help, which was granted on condition that Mary, Queen of Scots, should be sent to the French court for her education and eventual marriage to the Dauphin Francis, heir to King Henry II.

In May 1548 Mary departed for France, where she received the education of a renaissance princess. She learned French, Italian and Latin, and absorbed the automatic Catholicism of the French court. Her essentially pampered upbringing, however, left her less well equipped to rule Scotland than any of the five Jameses, who had learned political realities in a harder school. In 1558, at the age of sixteen, Mary married the Dauphin Francis, and by a secret agreement, ceded her kingdom to the Crown of France if she should die without issue. Scotland, saved from becoming a satellite of England, was pledged, under these circumstances, to become a satellite of France.

In the meantime, Mary of Guise had become Regent of Scotland in 1554, and Arran had received the French dukedom of Châtelherault, as a reward for stepping down for her. The Queen-Regent spent the rest of her life struggling to defend Scotland as a Catholic kingdom for her daughter to inherit. But ideology cannot be fought with the sword, and Scotland turned Protestant during the minority of Mary, Queen of Scots.

John Hamilton, Châtelherault's half-brother, who had succeeded Cardinal Beaton as Archbishop of St Andrews, attempted to organize the reform of the Catholic Church in Scotland from within. He held three Church Councils, in 1549, 1552 and 1559, which legislated against notorious abuses, and issued a new *Cathechism* which made some concessions to Lutheran doctrines. But his efforts were too little and too late in the face of the influence of a new wave of Protestantism, from Calvinist Geneva. Calvin's austere interpretation of Christianity made a stronger appeal to the Scottish character than had the Lutheranism which had been preached in the reign of James V. The stern doctrine of predestination, which declared that some men were eternally elected for salvation, and the rest were irretrievably damned, gave converts to Calvinism, with their consequent conviction of election, a sense of moral ascendancy which can scarcely be exaggerated.

Political encouragement came to the Scottish Protestants with the death of Henry II of France, in 1559. The young husband of Mary, Queen of Scots, became King Francis II, and it appeared improbable that the Queen-Consort of France would ever return to rule her native kingdom. The prospect of an absentee sovereign offered the Protestants the chance to seize the initiative, especially when the great Reformer John Knox returned from a period of exile in Geneva to inspire them. Suddenly the Queen-Regent faced an armed rebellion, headed by a group of noblemen who called themselves the 'Lords of the Congregation', amongst whom Lord James Stewart, the ablest of James V's bastards, played the leading part.

Mary of Guise was already a dying woman when the Reformation rebellion broke out. Her death in June 1560 saved her the humiliation of defeat, for the rebels triumphed with the help of Elizabeth I of England, who had occupied her throne for eighteen months. The victorious rebels summoned a parliament of dubious legality, which forbade the celebration of Mass in Scotland, repudiated the authority and jurisdiction of the Pope, and adopted a Protestant *Confession of*

Faith, which was the official foundation of the new Kirk. The transformation of Scotland, which had been long in preparation, seemed to have occurred almost overnight.

The Reformers, like many other revolutionaries, had ideals which were more easily postulated than put into practice. In the *First Book of Discipline* they set out a programme under which a high proportion of the wealth of the pre-Reformation Church was to finance the purposes of the new Kirk. The revenues of the bishops were to be diverted to the universities, and to the superintendents, who were to perform the bishops' administrative functions without enjoying their old powers; parochial revenues were to pay the stipends of ministers, provide for the poor, and be used to establish a school in every parish. These estimable plans were largely frustrated by the secular supporters of the Reformation, especially the nobles who already held lay abbacies, and 'greedily gripped' monastic lands at this unparalleled opportunity.

To the character of society the Reformation brought an unwonted austerity which was evoked in an elegiac verse by Sir Richard Maitland of Lethington, who remembered the brilliant court of James V, and the *joie de vivre* of his subjects:

> Quare is the blyithness that hes been
> Baith in burgh and landwart* seen?
> Amang lordis and ladyis schein,†
> Dauncing, singing, game and play:
> Bot now I wait†† nocht quhat thay mein,
> All mirriness is worn away . . .

*town and countryside
†brilliant
††know

Saints' days were no longer celebrated with processions. Christmas and Easter were no longer festivals. The collapse of the old Church was emphasized by the dilapidation of ecclesiastical buildings. In many instances the destruction begun by Henry VIII's army in the 'Rough Wooing' was completed by iconoclastic mobs in the Reformation rebellion. Scotland presented a dismal picture of post-war depression when Mary, Queen of Scots, returned in 1561.

At the end of 1560 Francis II of France unexpectedly died of an abscess in the ear, and Mary, deprived of a glorious future, found herself politically insignificant as a childless *reine douarière* of France. She resolved to take up the dangerous challenge of ruling her metamorphosed kingdom. There have been many conflicting interpretations of the character of Mary, Queen of Scots, but undoubtedly she possessed both courage and charm, and probably more of the legendary beauty attributed to her than most of her surviving portraits suggest.

Mary received good advice at the beginning of her personal rule from her half-brother Lord James Stewart, whom she created Earl of Moray, and from William Maitland of Lethington (son of the poet previously quoted) whom she appointed her Secretary of State. Both advised her to follow a conciliatory policy in religion: to practise Catholicism as her sovereign privilege, and officially to recognize the Reformed religion. Mary accepted their advice, and in the early years of her rule she prospered. Her ambition was to win recognition as the successor of Elizabeth I. As granddaughter of Margaret Tudor, Mary had a claim to the English throne which in Catholic eyes was superior to Elizabeth's, since Elizabeth, as the child of

Henry's marriage to Anne Boleyn, was from the Catholic viewpoint illegitimate. Elizabeth had no wish to recognize Mary's claim, but discussion of it was useful for purposes of diplomacy.

Mary's troubles arose from her choice of a husband. After negotiations with several European princes, Mary married her cousin, Henry Stuart, Lord Darnley, on 29 July 1565. Darnley was the grandson of Margaret Tudor by her second marriage to the Earl of Angus. Their daughter, Lady Margaret Douglas, married Matthew Stuart, fourth Earl of Lennox, a great-grandson of James II, so that Darnley had reversionary claims to the thrones of both Scotland and England. Genealogically, Mary made an intelligent choice, for the marriage of the two cousins would strengthen the claim of their children to the coveted English throne. Personally, however, the marriage was disastrous, for though Darnley was handsome and superficially attractive, he was arrogant and self-indulgent. Soon he made dangerous enemies, including the Queen's powerful half-brother Moray, and many other noblemen. Then he quarrelled with the Queen, and accused her of infidelity with her secretary, David Riccio.

On 9 March 1566 Darnley, with his kinsman James Douglas, fourth Earl of Morton, Lords Lindsay and Ruthven, and other conspirators, broke into the Queen's apartment in Holyroodhouse, and murdered Riccio, who was resented as an influential foreigner, and suspected of being a Papal agent. Mary, who was six months pregnant with the child begotten by Darnley before the Riccio scandal was invented, never forgave her husband for the murder committed in her presence, the danger to her life, or the slur on her reputation.

Mary's son James was born on 19 June 1566, and the birth of an heir made his degenerate father dispensable. Mary sought a means of escape from her intolerable marriage. In her disillusionment with Darnley she came to rely on James Hepburn, fourth Earl of Bothwell, who was a loyal though dangerously violent and amoral supporter. The Queen may have accepted the necessity of Darnley's death, if she were to be free of him without endangering the legitimacy of her son by a divorce. Darnley died on 10 February 1567, when the house in which he was sleeping, at Kirk o' Field, on the outskirts of Edinburgh, was blown up with an extravagant quantity of gunpowder. He himself was found dead in the garden, uninjured by the blast but murdered by strangulation. The extent of the Queen's complicity has remained controversial; Darnley had many enemies, but the chief suspect was Bothwell.

Mary, Queen of Scots, sacrificed her reputation when she married Bothwell on 15 May 1567, after he had been tried for the murder of Darnley and unconvincingly acquitted. The best explanation of her apparently insensate behaviour is that she was pregnant by Bothwell, and as she had been estranged from Darnley since the murder of Riccio, it would have been common knowledge that the child could not have been his. The fact that she miscarried of twins in July 1567 suggests that her marriage to Bothwell was a matter of necessity. The marriage caused a coalescence of opposition in the name of Prince James. Mary and Bothwell faced James's supporters on the Field of Carberry Hill, near Musselburgh, on 15 June, where they were defeated not in battle but by the desertion of their forces. Mary was taken as a captive to Edinburgh, and afterwards imprisoned in the island castle of Lochleven, where she was forced to abdicate in favour of her son, and to appoint the Earl of Moray as his Regent, on 24 July.

The following spring Mary made a dramatic escape from Lochleven, on 2 May 1568, and quickly gathered an army of supporters, headed by the Hamiltons. On 13 May she was defeated by the forces of the Regent Moray, at the Battle of Langside, near Glasgow. She fled across the Solway Firth, to seek refuge in England, in the hope that Elizabeth, who had shown sympathy for her during her captivity, would assist in her restoration. Elizabeth's actions spoke louder than her words, for she held Mary as a prisoner in England for the next nineteen years.

In the meantime, while Mary was imprisoned in Lochleven, James VI was crowned at the age of thirteen months, by newly devised Protestant rites. On the momentous occasion of the fusion of the Reformation and the monarchy, the sermon was preached by John Knox. Thenceforward James VI was kept in the safety of Stirling Castle, while civil war raged between his partisans and the remaining supporters of his mother. While the victory of the forces of the Reformation provided the background of his childhood, James was educated to become the ideal Protestant ruler. His tutor was a renowned Scottish scholar, George Buchanan, a dour sexagenarian who crammed him with Latin, Greek, Calvinist theology and propagandist history. James was taught that his mother was an adulteress and a murderess, and that subjects had the right to rebel against a tyrannous ruler. James absorbed Buchanan's scholarship, but rejected his political theory and his propaganda. He grew up to be impressively intellectual, and made his own contribution to political theory in *The Trew Law of Free Monarchies* (1598) and *Basilikon Doron* (1599), books which stressed the divine right of kings to rule, their moral responsibility to God, and their subjects' duty of obedience.

During the minority four regents in turn ruled Scotland: the Earl of Moray, who was assassinated in 1570; the Earl of Lennox, James's paternal grandfather, who was killed in a street-fight in Stirling in 1571; the Earl of Mar, James's guardian, who died of natural causes in 1572; and the Earl of Morton, who successfully imposed his authority for some years.

The grimness of James VI's adolescence was alleviated when his Franco-Scottish cousin Esmé Stuart d'Aubigny visited Scotland in 1579. Captivated by his charm, James expressed the first love of his life by showering his cousin with honours, culminating in the dukedom of Lennox, in 1581. Lennox and his henchman Captain James Stewart organized the downfall of Morton, by accusing him of participation in the murder of the King's father. Morton admitted foreknowledge of the crime, for which he was executed.

Lennox, as a Catholic, was suspected by the Kirk and the Protestant nobility of plotting the restoration of Mary, Queen of Scots. He attempted to allay suspicion by allowing the young King to convert him to Calvinism, and by signing the Negative Confession of 1581, a document which condemned a wide variety of Catholic doctrines; but in 1582 he was overthrown by a *coup d'état*, in which the King was seized by the fanatically Protestant first Earl of Gowrie. Lennox was driven from Scotland, and died in France the following year. James remained a captive for ten months, but like his predecessors he was ambitious to rule, and in June 1583 he overthrew his captors and asserted his authority, with the aid of Captain James Stewart, whom he created Earl of Arran.

Early in his personal rule, James revealed his preoccupation with the English succession. He was eager to win recognition as the successor of Elizabeth I, since it was now obvious that she would remain the 'Virgin Queen'. Elizabeth mistrusted Arran as an unprincipled adventurer, but after he had been overthrown in 1585, and a moderate administration formed under James's wise chancellor, John Maitland of Thirlestane, relations between Scotland and England grew more amicable. In 1586 an Anglo-Scottish treaty was signed, and though Elizabeth refused to grant James formal recognition as her heir, she began to pay him a pension of £4000 a year, and gave him some deliberately imprecise encouragement. But, almost immediately, there followed the revelation of Mary, Queen of Scots' complicity in the Babington Conspiracy to assassinate Elizabeth and enthrone Mary herself. James faced the dilemma of his obligation to defend his mother's life, and his desire to maintain his alliance with England.

James's attitude to his mother was ambivalent. He had rejected Buchanan's propaganda, yet he had never known her, and he could not love her. So long as she lived, his own position as King of Scots and unacknowledged heir of England was not unimpeachable. He had good reasons for hoping that she might predecease Elizabeth by natural causes. However, he protested strongly against her trial and execution, though he refused to break off diplomatic relations with England or to threaten military action. Mary went to her execution with exemplary fortitude on 8 February 1587 and many years later James honoured her memory and salved his conscience by giving her a magnificent tomb in Westminster Abbey.

Preoccupation with the English succession likewise dictated James's attitude to the Spanish Armada, in 1588. His official policy towards England was friendly neutrality, but he knew that the remaining Catholic nobles, led by the sixth Earl of Huntly for whom he felt affection, were corresponding with Philip II of Spain. In the event of a Spanish victory, James hoped that his favour to the Catholic interest might give him a chance of retaining his throne. But the threatened crisis was diverted by the defeat of the Armada, and the Anglo-Scottish treaty remained unbroken.

In 1589 James VI was secure enough to leave Scotland for several months, when he sailed to Oslo to marry Anne of Denmark, a Protestant princess of his own choice. The marriage, though briefly idyllic, was ultimately disappointing. Anne was a blonde Scandinavian beauty, and not highly educated, while James was an intellectual with homosexual preferences which grew more marked in later life. But despite their discrepancy of character, they produced seven children, three of whom survived infancy: Henry, who died in 1612; Elizabeth, the future Queen of Bohemia and ancestress of the House of Hanover; and Charles, the future Charles I.

During the later years of James VI's reign in Scotland his principal concerns were the relations between Kirk and State and the imposing of law and order; while constantly in the background was his abiding preoccupation with the English succession.

Under the leadership of Andrew Melville, on whom the mantle of John Knox had fallen, the Kirk took on its characteristic Presbyterian organization of a hierarchy of ecclesiastical courts: Kirk Sessions, Presbyteries, Synods, and the all-powerful General Assembly which, like Parliament, contained representatives of the Three Estates. Melville, taking his cue from Calvinist Geneva, claimed that the Scottish Kirk was a theocratic organization, divinely empowered to direct the secular government. James VI, though doctrinally Calvinist, was no Presbyterian. He was convinced that the divine right to rule was vested in the King, who was head of both Kirk and State, and he was determined to control the Kirk through bishops, as the agents of the royal authority. Melville and his supporters insisted on the parity of ministers, and Melville also told James, 'There are two Kings and two Kingdoms in Scotland. There is Christ Jesus the King, and His Kingdom the Kirk; whose subject King James the Sixth is, and of whose Kingdom not a king, nor a lord, nor a head, but a member.' On the same occasion Melville declared that the King was merely 'God's sillie vassal' (i.e., simple servant). James responded with his famous dictum, 'No Bishop, no King', and in the end he was victorious, and his bishops became Crown servants who assisted in the task of keeping order in the outlying areas of the kingdom.

After a double ration of disorder, resulting from a royal minority and the upheaval of the Reformation, the task of reimposing law and order might have appeared insuperable. Certain violent incidents highlight the King's difficulties: for example, Huntly's murder of the 'Bonny Earl of Moray' in 1592. James was known to favour the Catholic Huntly, and he suffered much opprobrium because Moray was a Protestant, and popular. A ballad suggested the King's interest in the murder:

> ... the Bonny Earl o' Moray,
> O, he was the Queen's love.

James endured a sustained series of trials in the attempted *coups d'état* of his unbalanced cousin, Francis, Earl of Bothwell, who was a nephew of Mary's Bothwell, and an illegitimate grandson of James V. Bothwell may have aspired to the throne, but his attempts concurrently to use the support of the Kirk, the friendship of Huntly, and the powers of darkness – supposedly at the command of the 'North Berwick Witches' – led to his downfall. He was forced to leave Scotland in 1595, and he died in Naples in 1612. The last attempt to subvert James VI's government was the mysterious 'Gowrie Plot' of 1600, which may have been an attempt to assassinate the King.

It would be easy to represent James VI's reign in Scotland merely as a series of dramatic incidents, yet these incidents were in reality only interruptions of the King's sustained and mainly successful efforts to improve the administration of his kingdom, and the quality of life for his subjects. The fulfilment of his achievement, however, belongs to the second half of his reign, after his accession to the throne of England.

Elizabeth I died in March 1603, by which time James had been in correspondence with her chief minister, Robert Cecil, for two years. The way for his accession had been made smooth, and whether or not Elizabeth at the last yielded to the determination of a lifetime and designated James as her successor would have made little difference. James VI of Scotland was proclaimed James I of England, and joyfully accepted by the southern kingdom, which had feared the warfare that had so often followed a disputed succession.

Such a conclusion would have been unforeseeable during the centuries of struggle in which Scottish independence had been with difficulty defended against English aggression; but time would show that the Union of Crowns of 1603 did not provide a happy ending to that struggle.

CHAPTER SIX

A Kingdom Without a King
1603 – 1707

King James VI of Scotland, firmly established as James I of England, wrote: 'This I may say for Scotland, and may truly vaunt it: here I sit and govern it with my pen. I write and it is done, and by a Clerk of the Council I govern Scotland now, which others could not do by the sword.' This boast underestimated the achievements of his ancestors, but it accurately represented his own.

Unfortunately for Scotland, the King's success in governing with his pen created a precedent for absentee monarchy. When James left Scotland he promised to return once every three years; the promise was sincere, but financial and organizational pressures made it impossible to fulfil. However, a system of posts connecting London and Edinburgh carried his instructions to the Scottish Privy Council, and to the Parliamentary Committee, 'The Lords of the Articles', through which he controlled the Scottish Parliament.

James did not imagine that in leaving Scotland he had left a completed task. Of the continuing problems that of keeping order in the Borders was spontaneously, if not instantaneously, solved by the Union of Crowns. Disorder was condemned to a natural death when malefactors could no longer find protection by crossing a frontier. Ideally, James would have abolished any demarcation by creating a United Kingdom, of which the Borders would have become the 'Middle Shires'. He did his best to foster the identity of the United Kingdom by referring to his kingdoms as 'Great Britain'. But his views were unwelcome in England, and though the Scottish Parliament passed an Act of Union in 1607, the English Parliament refused to follow suit. One hundred years later, in circumstances less favourable to Scotland, the Union took place; but if the Union was indeed desirable, 1607 would have been a date more advantageous to Scotland, for then the Union would have been the work of a Scots king, the welfare of whose countrymen was close to his heart. The best concession to unity which James could secure from the English Parliament was that subjects born after the Union of Crowns (the *post-nati*) should possess dual nationality.

A more long-standing problem of unification, that of the Highlands and the Lowlands, unsolved by James VI's predecessors, continued to preoccupy him after his removal to England. The old dichotomy of the kingdom had been increased during the fifteenth and sixteenth centuries by social and economic changes in the Lowlands which the Highlands had not shared. The Lowlands contained all the universities: St Andrews (1413), Glasgow (1451), Aberdeen (1495)* and Edinburgh (1582). All the greater medieval ecclesiastical foundations had been in the Lowlands, and after the Reformation the Highlands were for a long time as much neglected by the Kirk as they had been by the Roman Church. The royal residences, occupied in turn by the peripatetic court, were in the Lowlands:

---

*Marischal College, Aberdeen (1593) had the status of a separate university.

Edinburgh Castle, Holyroodhouse, Stirling Castle, and the palaces of Linlithgow, Falkland and Dunfermline. The principal burghs were all south-east of the Highland Line: Edinburgh, Glasgow, St Andrews, Perth, Dundee and Aberdeen. Inverness was the only considerable burgh in the Highlands. This concentration of intellectual, ecclesiastical, governmental and commercial life in the south-eastern division of Scotland left the Highlands free to develop their well-established separatism.

Highland life did not stagnate. The balance of power between the clans was constantly shifting, sometimes as a result of internecine strife, sometimes as a result of government intervention. For example, the suppression and annexation of the Lordship of the Isles made way for the rise of the Clan Campbell, at first as the agent of royal authority, later as a greater rival to it than the Lordship of the Isles had ever been. In his attempt to discipline the Highlands, James VI did not hesitate to use the only method which had been available to his ancestors, that of employing one clan to quell another, and by 'Letters of Fire and Sword' authorizing the clan selected as the government's agent to extirpate disorderly neighbours. In 1603, shortly before James's accession to the English throne, there was a clan battle between the MacGregors and the Colquhouns in Glen Fruin, only twelve miles from Dumbarton. The MacGregors slew 140 of their enemies, and only suffered two losses, whereupon James took the unprecedented step of attempting to extirpate the offending clan by outlawing the MacGregors and forbidding the future use of their surname. In general, however, James preferred to discipline the clans by applying the more civilized principle of the

'General Band', whereby a chief was made responsible for the good behaviour of his clansmen.

In seeking to bring order to the Western Isles James made use of Bishop Andrew Knox, who in 1609 was instrumental in persuading a group of chiefs to sign the 'Statutes of Iona' in which, amongst other measures, they bound themselves to dispense with the services of their bards, who had kept alive the memories of ancient feuds, and to send their sons for education in the Lowlands. Both these measures were directed against the separatist influence of the Gaelic language. James VI, who had been educated in the traditions of European scholarship, could not have been expected to see that it would have been more constructive to comprehend Gaelic culture in his ideal of a unified Scotland, rather than to attempt to eradicate it.

In the Northern Isles the principal agent of the King's authority was Bishop James Law, who was effective in ending the tyrannous rule of James's illegitimate cousin, Patrick Stewart, Earl of Orkney, the notorious 'Earl Pate', who was executed in Edinburgh in 1615. Gradually James VI increased the number and the powers of the Scottish bishops. By 1610 there were eleven bishops and two archbishops, whose chief opponent, Andrew Melville, had been summoned to London in 1606, and imprisoned in the Tower for three years. On his release, Melville was forbidden to return to Scotland, but was permitted to accept a chair at the University of Sedan. In this way James avoided making a martyr of him, and proceeded cautiously to bring about as great a degree of conformity between the Scottish Kirk and the Church of England as was practically possible in the interests of the unification of his kingdoms.

As the years passed, James's appreciation of Scottish public opinion grew less exact, as was illustrated when he paid his only return visit to Scotland in 1617. He used his visit to advance the anglicanization of the Kirk, by introducing the 'Five Articles of Perth', which decreed that Holy Communion should be received kneeling, that Confirmation should be administered by bishops, not ministers; that the Kirk should celebrate the festivals of the Christian Year; and that private Baptism and Communion should be permitted in cases of serious sickness. These seemingly moderate requirements appeared to the Kirk to suggest a 'popish' attitude to sacraments and festivals. The Presbyterian clergy and many of the laity resisted vehemently. King James successfully demanded that the General Assembly, which met at Perth in 1618, should adopt the Five Articles; but having won his victory in principle, he did not enquire too closely how far the Articles were adopted in practice. His single return to Scotland served to remind him that though his countrymen could often be manipulated, they could seldom be coerced. King James VI died on 27 March 1625, a few months short of his fifty-ninth birthday. His long reign had given Scotland an increase of law and order, and a happy respite from the troubles which had attended the Reformation; as religio-political strife revived in the course of the seventeenth century, James's reputation grew in retrospect. Scotland remembered him as 'Blessed King James'.

He was succeeded by his second son, Charles, who had been born in Dunfermline Palace in 1600. Charles's English subjects did not forget his Scottish birth, which made him as foreign as his father. Yet to the Scots he was equally foreign, for he had lived in

England since shortly after the Union of Crowns, and his knowledge of Scotland derived only from expatriate Scots at the English court. Charles developed into a man of reserved character, and a very much less flexible ruler than his father, whose appreciation of the limits of the possible he never acquired.

Charles I saw his duty as the completion of his father's policy to anglicize the Scottish Kirk, but whereas James's preference for episcopacy and desire for religious conformity originated in political considerations, Charles's inspiration was singlemindedly religious. To him, Presbyterianism was merely an erroneous subspecies of Protestantism; Anglicanism was the purer form, which it was his duty to establish, by force if necessary. As a preliminary measure to making a proper provision for the Church in Scotland as he envisaged it, Charles issued an Act of Revocation in 1625. It had been the custom of the Kings of Scots to revoke all grants made during their minorities when they reached the age of twenty-five, which was a reasonable measure since the grants of minors might have been made under duress. But Charles's act was exceptionally sweeping as it revoked all grants made since 1540, thus including post-Reformation grants of Church lands. By this act Charles alienated a large section of the Scottish nobility – the so-called 'Lords of Erection', whose titles derived from secularized Church lands – and he did not gain the support of the Kirk, to which his anglicizing policy was already suspect.

In 1633 Charles I paid his first visit to Scotland since he had left it as a small child. He was crowned King of Scots in the Chapel Royal of Holyrood with full Anglican ritual, and following his visit Edinburgh was created a Bishopric with the High Kirk of St Giles as its Cathedral. But Charles, far from impressing the Scots with the 'beauty of holiness' which he loved, aroused in the Kirk and its adherents a renewed dread of 'popery'. Ill-advisedly in these inflammatory circumstances, Charles I and his new Archbishop of Canterbury, William Laud, decided to reshape the Scottish liturgy. From their viewpoint it was a gesture of adaptability to acknowledge that Scotland and England required different liturgies. The *Revised Prayer Book* designed for Scotland, in the composition of which the opinion of Scottish bishops was consulted, has been praised for its dignity of language; but despite its careful use of the word 'presbyter' instead of 'priest', it was an alien importation, which made it unacceptable. Its inauguration in St Giles, on 23 July 1637, was the occasion of a well-organized riot. Charles I, who was not present, did not understand the seriousness of the reaction. He ordered the use of the *Revised Prayer Book* to be enforced throughout Scotland.

The use of force invited resistance. In the autumn of 1637 a committee known as 'the Tables' was formed to combat the King's anglicanizing policy. James Graham, fifth Earl of Montrose, Archibald Campbell, eighth Earl of Argyll, and many other noblemen, with lairds, lawyers and ministers joined in resisting the innovations. Charles, far more out of touch with Scottish opinion than his father had ever been, had ignored this opposition. Charles's refusal to understand the strength of feeling which his policy had aroused, led to the signing of the National Covenant, on 28 September 1638. The Covenant, signed by nobility, clergy and commons, was regarded by its most fervent signatories as a direct contract between Scotland and God. 'Scotland is the Betrothed Virgin: we were espoused to Jesus Christ and joined to Him by a marriage contract, never to be forgotten.' Charles I, a devout and sincere man, could never understand that the devoutness and sincerity of others could lead them to hold a faith as intransigent as his own.

The National Covenant would have been less powerful had it been merely an expression of religious fanaticism; but it owed much to the legal skill of Archibald Johnston of Wariston, a lawyer whose perfervid religion did not prevent him from drafting a rational document. Its preamble was the Negative Confession of 1581, which had condemned a wide range of Catholic doctrines. It asserted a desire for a Presbyterian ecclesiastical polity, rejected Anglican innovations, and pledged loyalty to the King. The Covenant appealed to a wide range of potential signatories, from fanatical to moderate opponents of the King's policy; this proved to be its initial strength and its ultimate weakness.

In a tardy attempt to resolve his differences with this vigorous opposition, Charles permitted a General Assembly of the Kirk to meet at Glasgow, in November 1638 (the first General Assembly since 1618). The King sent the Duke of Hamilton to preside, as his Commissioner, but he instructed Hamilton to 'flatter them with what hopes you please ... until I be ready to suppress them.' Hamilton soon realized that the time for offering flattering hopes was past. He walked out of the Assembly, which thereafter deposed and excommunicated the Scottish bishops, and repudiated the *Revised Prayer Book*. Thenceforward, the King could only hope to impose his religious policy by force.

The next two years witnessed the so-called 'Bishops' Wars'. The first involved no fighting, and ended with the unsatisfactory Pacification of Berwick, by which it was agreed that the disputes between the King and the Covenanters should be referred to a new General Assembly and Scottish Parliament. Both these bodies refused to compromise, and the Second Bishops' War followed. The Covenanters had by now gained the services of a distinguished general, Alexander Leslie, who had fought for Sweden in the Thirty Years' War, and he in turn was supported by the natural military genius of the young Earl of Montrose. Charles I's army of reluctant recruits was easily defeated.

By this time Charles I was involved in much more than a religious confrontation with the Scots. He could not afford warfare without recourse to the English Parliament, but Parliament had not met since 1629, and it had a long list of grievances against the King and his ministers. The Long Parliament, which first met in 1640, impeached Charles's most able ministers, the Earl of Strafford and Archbishop Laud. The King was unable to save the life of Strafford, and the outbreak of Civil War became a possibility. In this extremity, Charles resolved to sink his differences with the Covenanters, and seek help in Scotland. He visited Edinburgh in the autumn of 1641, accepted the decisions of the General Assembly of 1638 to abolish episcopacy and reject the *Revised Prayer Book*, granted the Scottish Parliament the right (which it had already arrogated) of challenging the actions of his ministers, and endeavoured to purchase the support of erstwhile opponents, by creating Alexander Leslie Earl of Leven, and raising Argyll to the title of Marquess. Charles's moves were transparently opportunist, and his concessions were too late to win goodwill. They were, as a contemporary observed, 'to-day that which would have absolutely satisfied yesterday, and the next day that which would have satisfied this day . . . it was ever his constant unhappiness to give nothing in time.'

Civil War broke out in England in 1642, partly as a result of Charles's reluctance to make concessions to his opponents, and partly as a result of his bad faith when he was obliged to do so. The Royalists were victorious in the early stages of the war; the Parliamentarians, in their turn, solicited Scottish help. The result of these negotiations was the Solemn League and Covenant, signed on 25 September 1643. In return for a promised payment of £30,000 a month, the Scottish Parliament agreed to make war against the King, on condition that Presbyterianism should be established in England and Ireland. Charles I experienced the reverse of his own policy when the Covenanters entered the Civil War for religious reasons; much as they had objected to his attempt to anglicanize Scotland, they saw their own religious duty in equally intransigent terms when they sought to presbyterianize Great Britain.

The English Parliament honoured the Solemn League and Covenant by summoning the Westminster Assembly of Divines, to establish the agreed uniformity of worship. It was a predominantly English gathering, with a membership of over one hundred, attended by eight Scottish delegates. However, the Westminster Confession of Faith, the Larger and Shorter Catechisms, the Directory of Public Worship and the Form of Church Government produced by this assembly were adopted by the Scottish Parliament and the General Assembly.

The army of the Covenanters invaded England early in 1644, and played a decisive part in the defeat of the Royalists at Marston Moor, in July. But as a counterpoise the Royalist cause in Scotland revived when Montrose resolved to fight for the King. Montrose, whom Charles I gratefully created Marquess, had had many bitter differences with Argyll, besides which he did not forget that the Covenant contained a pledge of loyalty to the King. He raised an Irish and Highland army for the King's cause, and won a spectacular series of victories against Argyll and the extremist Covenanters at Tippermuir, Aberdeen, Inverlochy, Auldearn, Alford, and Kilsyth before he was defeated at Philiphaugh, in September 1645. In the meantime, Charles had been defeated at the Battle of Naseby, the decisive blow to the Royalist cause in England. Montrose did not despair, but Charles recognized that he had reached the end of his resources. In 1646 he surrendered to the Scottish army in England, at Newark. He was obliged to promise that Montrose would disband his army and leave Britain, and Montrose had no choice but to obey.

King Charles's situation was not completely hopeless, had he been able to see it. The Parliamentarian army, reorganized by Oliver Cromwell, increased in power at the expense of Parliament itself, and was far ~~~~~~~~~~~~~ to Presbyterianism. Intimidated by the army, the English Parliament defaulted on the Solemn League and Covenant. When Charles surrendered to the Scots they were deeply dissatisfied: they had not received the agreed payment, and England and

Ireland were no nearer to becoming Presbyterian. If Charles had promised what Parliament had failed to perform, even at this late stage the army of the Covenanters would have fought for him. But Charles refused to compromise, and so the Covenanters, to whom his presence was a considerable embarrassment, handed him over to the English, and returned to Scotland, after having received £400,000 arrears of pay. It appeared that they had done nothing other than sell the King.

Charles was confined, though not rigorously, on the Isle of Wight, and the more moderate Covenanters, shocked by the transaction at Newark, sent emissaries to him to reach a new agreement. This time Charles recognized his last chance, and true to the previously quoted estimate of his character, he gave 'to-day that which would have absolutely satisfied yesterday'. He agreed to introduce Presbyterianism to England for a trial period of three years. This agreement was known as the 'Engagement', and the 'Engagers' hastened back to Scotland to initiate a new war on the King's behalf.

In 1648 a Scottish army led by the Duke of Hamilton invaded England, to be defeated by Cromwell at Preston. The failure of the Engagement was fatal to the King. Charles I was tried before a tribunal which could not claim to be legally constituted, and executed on 30 January 1649. In Scotland the news of his execution was received with horror. To fight against the King was permissible, to execute him after a travesty of justice was impermissible. Montrose, who fainted when the news was brought to him in Brussels, wrote Charles I a noble epitaph, concluding,

I'll tune thy elegies to trumpet-sounds,
And write thy epitaph in blood and wounds.

Both Montrose and Argyll offered their services to
Charles I's eldest son, and Argyll had him proclaimed
King Charles II, in Edinburgh. Charles II was the first
king of his dynasty to have been born outside Scotland.
He was born in London, at St James's Palace, on 24
May 1630, the eldest child of Charles I's French
Queen, Henrietta Maria, whose proselytizing Cath-
olicism did so much to make her husband's ritualistic
Anglicanism seem the more 'popish' to Scottish
Covenanters and English Puritans. The future Charles
II was twelve at the outbreak of the Civil War. When
the Royalist cause faced defeat his father ordered him
to leave the country; in 1646 he took refuge first in
Jersey and then in France. This early experience of
exile developed the opportunism of his character.

Charles II accordingly accepted the services of both
Montrose and Argyll, knowing that they were enemies, but determined to use both of them to advance
his cause. Montrose invaded northern Scotland by way
of Orkney, with a mixed force of foreign mercenaries
and Orcadian recruits, but he failed to repeat his
previous achievements. He was defeated in Carbisdale,
and betrayed into the hands of Argyll by Macleod of
Assynt. Argyll had a series of humiliations to avenge,
and he was not prepared to forget them in the interests
of the new King. It was he who ensured that Montrose
should be tried for treason to the Covenant, and
executed on 21 May 1650. At the last Montrose
expressed his loyalty to the Covenant: 'The Covenant
which I took, I own it and adhere to it. Bishops, I care
not for them. I never intended to advance their

interests.' With the death of a heroic champion of incompatible causes, Charles II was forced to rely upon the fanatical 'Solemn-leaguers', who nonetheless retained the old Scottish attachment to monarchy.

In the summer of 1650 Charles II arrived in Scotland, powerless to resist whatever demands should be made of him, if he hoped to regain his kingdoms. He acquiesced in signing both the National Covenant and the Solemn League and Covenant, committing himself and his kingdoms to a form of religion with which he had no more sympathy than his father. Probably he never had any intention of abiding by the Covenants which he had signed under duress; some years later he expressed the opinion that 'Presbytery was not a religion for gentlemen'. But, pliant opportunist that he was, he became a Covenanted King, and was crowned at Scone on New Year's Day 1651, the crown being placed upon his head by Argyll.

In the meantime, Cromwell had invaded Scotland, and won a victory at Dunbar. But the newly crowned Charles boldly entered England, hoping to win support as he marched south. Cromwell pursued him and on 3 September 1651 he defeated Charles at Worcester. Charles, a closely hunted fugitive, managed to escape to France, to a second exile which lasted for nine years.

The victorious Cromwell imposed a Treaty of Union upon Scotland and England, and established in Scotland an efficient military government which had to be maintained by high taxation, and was consequently unpopular. The standard of law and order was impressive, as was the quality of justice, but the means were too much detested for the results to be appreciated. The Restoration of 1660, which restored both the

King and Scotland's status as a separate kingdom, was greeted with general rejoicing.

Charles II returned to England in May, a week before his thirtieth birthday, but neither then nor thereafter did he revisit Scotland. Though Charles I's experiment in absentee monarchy had scarcely been encouraging, Charles II still preferred to imitate his grandfather in governing Scotland with his pen. Charles II's memories of his experiences as a Covenanted King did not inspire his gratitude. Though he was in general sparing in acts of vengeance, he exacted the life of Argyll who, after he had crowned Charles had gone on to collaborate with Cromwell. Argyll, a strict Calvinist, who was doubtless confident of his place among the elect, said before his execution, 'I set the crown on the King's head, he hastens me now to a better crown than his.'

Charles II's chief agent of authority in Scotland was John Maitland, second Earl and first Duke of Lauderdale, who had been one of the Scottish delegates at the Westminster Assembly, and later one of the Engagers. Though he was grasping and corrupt, he was far more able than any of the Scots who had administered Scotland for Charles I. Through Lauderdale Charles II controlled the Scottish Privy Council; the Scottish Parliament was controlled as it had been under James VI, through the 'Lords of the Articles'.

The Restoration Parliament of 1661, which was known as the 'Drunken Parliament', rescinded all legislation passed since 1633. This had the effect of restoring episcopacy, and of reviving the pre-Covenant system of patronage, whereby a minister of the Kirk was appointed by the local laird and not by his congregation. Ill-advisedly, a new enactment required all ministers appointed since 1649 to resign their livings and seek reappointment by their legal patrons. A substantial minority of ministers could not reconcile their consciences to this measure. About three hundred ministers, approximately one third of the total number, refused to comply, preferring to be deprived of their manses and their livings. These resolute men, determined to uphold both the spirit and the letter of the Covenant, enjoyed the support of their congregations, who soon began to attend 'Conventicles', or illegal services, in farm buildings and in lonely places out of doors.

The Government reacted with severity; Conventicles were dispersed by armed force, and heavy fines were imposed on those who attended them. But repression served merely to inflame the Covenanters' ardour. The fiercest resistance to Government policy came from the south-west of Scotland: Ayrshire, Lanarkshire, Dumfriesshire and Galloway. In 1666 the Covenanters of the south-west marched on Edinburgh, where they were routed at Rullion Green, on the outskirts of the city. The executions of the leaders, which took place in Edinburgh, Glasgow and Ayr, were intended to deter sympathizers from taking arms; but they were ill-judged, for they provided the Covenanters with a first group of martyrs.

Lauderdale, who had a residual sympathy for Presbyterianism, tried a policy of appeasement, but his Declaration of Indulgence, which offered the expelled ministers a chance to resume their livings on compromise terms, elicited little response, and a repressive policy was resumed. In the later years of Charles II's reign an unhappy situation deteriorated even further. In 1679 Archbishop Sharp of St Andrews was mur-

dered by a group of Covenanters, and against all
likelihood, a Government force commanded by John
Graham of Claverhouse, a kinsman of Montrose, was
defeated by Covenanters in a skirmish at Drumclog.
Charles II sent his illegitimate son, the Duke of
Monmouth, to restore order, and Monmouth defeated
the Covenanters at Bothwell Bridge. Severe reprisals
followed. Twelve hundred prisoners were confined
out of doors, in Greyfriars Churchyard in Edinburgh.
About two thirds of them obtained their release, by
taking an oath of submission, but the remainder
accepted the sufferings of exposure and of sentences of
death or transportation to penal servitude in the West
Indies for the sake of their convictions.

The sufferings of a small number of Covenanters
from a limited area of Scotland earned for the later
years of Charles II's reign the bitter name of 'the
Killing Time'. The influence of this unhappy episode
was out of all proportion to its small scope and
duration. Charles II did not live to see the conclusion,
for he died in 1685. During his reign Scotland had
suffered increasingly from the effects of absentee
monarchy, for Charles II was basically out of sympathy with the Scottish problems which he had
inherited. The history of his unhappy relations with
the Covenanters is the more discreditable to him, in
that in other contexts he showed himself to be a
basically tolerant man.

Since Charles II's Portuguese Queen, Catherine of
Braganza, had failed to bear children, he was succeeded by his brother, James, Duke of York, who had
been born in 1633. Charles had been a crypto-Catholic
for much of his life, and was received into the Catholic
Church on his deathbed. James was converted to

Catholicism by his first wife, Anne Hyde, daughter of the Earl of Clarendon, who was herself a convert. Anne Hyde bore James two daughters, Mary and Anne, who were brought up in the Anglican faith. James, after his first wife's death, married a second Catholic bride, Mary of Modena, who for some years failed to produce a living child.

The accession of James VII of Scotland and II of England gave Scotland its first Catholic sovereign since Mary, Queen of Scots, and England its first since Mary I ('Bloody Mary'), neither of whom offered an encouraging precedent. James VII was not a complete stranger to Scotland. In 1679 he had succeeded Lauderdale as Charles II's Commissioner in Scotland, and he had spent two periods of residence there: the winter of 1679, and a longer period from October 1680 to March 1682. James had made himself agreeable to the Scots on these occasions, but after his accession his religious views gained the upper hand, when he believed that he possessed the power to enforce them. Years later, his *Memoirs*, referring to him in the third person, contained the following illuminating passage:

> ... If he had agreed to live quietly and treat his religion as a private matter ... he could have been one of the most powerful Kings ever to reign in England ... but, having been called by Almighty God to rule these kingdoms, he would think of nothing but the propagation of the Catholic religion ... for which he has been and always would be willing to sacrifice everything, regardless of any merely temporal consideration.

These words provide the essential explanation of the brevity of James VII and II's reign.

In Scotland, on the accession of James VII, the political power of the Covenanters had been broken, though a broadly based preference for Presbyterianism remained. At first the King enjoyed the support of the victorious Episcopalians, who recognized their dependence on the monarchy. If James VII had been content to regard his Catholicism as a matter of personal conviction, he might have established such a *modus vivendi* as had existed during the later years of James VI: an ecclesiastical polity which has been described as 'Bishops-in-Presbytery', and a form of worship which contented all but an extremist minority. However, in Scotland as in England, James VII brought about his own downfall by his propagation of his own faith.

James's policy in Scotland was to establish a Catholic ascendancy through the conversion of men of influence, and to secure toleration for his Catholic subjects (of whom, according to a Roman envoy writing in 1677, there were only two thousand between the Solway and the Moray Firth, though Catholic clans survived in the Western Highlands). But the King's few converts were inspired by ambition rather than conviction, and the Parliament of 1686 firmly refused to grant toleration to Catholics. James fell back upon the use of the Royal Prerogative to carry out his unpopular policy. In August 1686 James granted freedom of worship to Catholics in private houses. In February 1687 he extended toleration to Quakers, and in June 1687, in an attempt to counter the unpopularity of his previous measures, James granted toleration to Presbyterians.

Contrary to the King's expectations, the extension

of toleration failed to reduce anti-Catholic feeling; instead, it raised alarm among many of the King's previous supporters. The Episcopalians, who had hitherto relied upon the support of the Crown, saw in toleration for the Presbyterians a withdrawal of royal support. The Presbyterians, naturally, found renewed courage. Many, who had conformed by attending Episcopalian parish churches, left them again to attend their own services of worship, now legally permitted within doors; others, who had preferred to leave the country, now returned from Holland, where they had found refuge. Their chosen place of exile was significant. James VII's elder daughter Mary was married to the Dutch Prince William of Orange, who was himself a grandson of Charles I. William, a Protestant of Stuart descent, married to a Stuart princess, was an acceptable alternative to James VII for those who found a Catholic monarchy unendurable. The birth of a son to Mary of Modena, on 10 June 1688, sealed the fate of James VII and II: in both Scotland and England a Catholic king might be endured as a temporary anomaly, but the prospect of a Catholic dynasty was not to be tolerated.

The 'Glorious Revolution' of 1688 was the work of English opponents of James's Catholicizing policy; but anti-Catholic sentiment made Scotland willing to participate in the overthrow of James VII. William of Orange landed at Torbay on 5 November 1688, and the following month James fled to France. William III and Mary II were crowned as joint sovereigns on 11 April 1689 (William was in fact William II of Scotland since only one previous King of Scots, William the Lion, had borne the same name, but William of Orange did not assume the style of William II and III).

The new King and Queen were undoubtedly usurpers, as they had supplanted a sovereign of indisputable legality and displaced the direct heir, Prince James Francis Edward, the son of James VII and Mary of Modena. Nonetheless, they were welcomed in both Scotland and England as deliverers of both kingdoms from the threat of 'popery'.

In Scotland, as in England, the 'Revolution Settlement' was intended to redefine the relations of Church and State. The Scottish Revolution Settlement, negotiated between April 1689 and June 1690, established Presbyterianism as the official religion of Scotland, abolished episcopacy, and freed Parliament to a great extent from royal control – much against King William's wishes – by the abolition of the Lords of the Articles. The Revolution Settlement was moderate and statesmanlike, but it could not be universally pleasing. Extremist Covenanters were dissatisfied because Presbyterianism was defined on the basis of an Act dating from the reign of James VI, not on that of the National Covenant, and because William was an 'Uncovenanted King'. Disaffected sectarians remained aloof from the new establishment. At the opposite extreme, the defeated Episcopalians tended to revert to their former loyalty, and many became 'Jacobites', or supporters of the exiled James VII, and later of his son and grandson.

Despite the ease with which James VII had been thrown, his supporters did not give up so easily. Catholics – principally Highlanders – Episcopalians and supporters of the legitimist principle made a strong enough Jacobite party to resist King William. The Catholic Duke of Gordon attempted to hold Edinburgh Castle for James VII, but was obliged to surrender it in June 1689. The following month Graham of Claverhouse, now Viscount Dundee, emulated Montrose, and raised a Highland army to regain Scotland for its rightful King. He defeated King William's troops at the Battle of Killiecrankie, but was killed at the moment of victory. The Jacobites were unable to replace him with a commander of equal ability, and until James VII's son reached maturity, Jacobite fortunes were in eclipse. There is a remarkable parallel between the careers of the loyalist champions, Montrose and Dundee: both were inspired by loyalty to the monarchist principle, and lost their lives in defence of it; both were unfortunate in the inadequacy of the kings to whom their services were given.

King William secured his victory by building Fort William, to establish control over the Highlands, and he demanded an oath of allegiance from the Jacobite chiefs, to be sworn by 1 January 1692. The degree of William's responsibility for what followed remains controversial. He may have accepted the advice of his Secretary of State, Sir John Dalrymple, Master of Stair, that to make an example of some Jacobite Highlanders might dispose the rest to abide by the oath submissively. James VII authorized his adherents to swear the oath to William; but one of them, a suitable victim for Stair's purpose, was fatefully late to do so.

MacIan MacDonald of Glencoe, whose clansmen had a record of disorder as well as of Jacobitism, was three days late in reaching Inveraray, where the oath was to be sworn to the Sheriff-depute; the latter was absent when he arrived, but he waited, and took the oath on 6 January. Lateness might have been overlooked, if good faith had been accepted. However, Stair had selected MacDonald of Glencoe as an example, and King William signed the order to extirpate him and his clansmen. In extenuation of William's action, it has been claimed that he may have signed the order without reading its contents.

The notorious Massacre of Glencoe was carried out on 13 February 1692, by a company of the Earl of Argyll's Regiment of Foot, commanded by Captain Robert Campbell of Glenlyon. Though the Campbells were hereditary enemies of the MacDonalds, since the soldiers were quartered on them, the MacDonalds gave them hospitality. Some days of fraternizing preceded the massacre. When it was ordered, in the small hours of the morning, some of the soldiers, disgusted by their orders, warned the prospective victims, many of whom therefore escaped. Thirty-eight men, women and children were killed, out of an intended total of one hundred and forty, but the victims included MacDonald of Glencoe and his wife, whose rings were gnawed from her fingers by her killers. The extremes of pity and savagery were extraordinarily demonstrated by Glenlyon's troops. The Massacre of Glencoe aroused a sense of outrage throughout Scotland, not because of the numbers involved, but because of the cold-blooded and dishonourable manner in which it had been planned. The reputation of William and his government was never redeemed.

Another unhappy episode – this time a commercial disaster – increased his unpopularity. After the relatively satisfactory settlement of Scotland's religious affairs which had followed the Revolution, the patriot and anti-Unionist Andrew Fletcher of Saltoun wrote 'By an unforeseen change in the genius of the Nation, all their thoughts and inclinations seemed to be turned upon trade.' In 1695 the Scottish Parliament passed an

Act to form a Company of Scotland trading to Africa and the Indies. The Scots were eager to break the monopoly of the English East India Company; but the English Parliament, in which the East India Company was powerfully represented, forbade English participation in the Scottish enterprise. The Scots were not discouraged. They replanned the scheme as a colonial venture, and resolved to found a Scots colony in Darien (the Isthmus of Panama) which offered the advantage of providing an easy point of contact between the Atlantic and Pacific Oceans.

Unfortunately for the future of the enterprise Darien was claimed by the Crown of Spain, and William III was anxious to retain Spanish goodwill, as his enemy Louis XIV of France was advancing French claims to the Spanish succession. Opposing both the commercial interest of England and the political interests of the King, the Scots raised the necessary capital, and in November 1698 the first expedition sailed for Darien, with insufficient provisions and an unsuitable cargo. Two further expeditions followed, and each in turn came to grief. Defeated by fever, starvation and Spanish hostility, the few survivors struggled home in 1700. For colonial failure, loss of two thousand lives, and loss of £300,000 of Scottish investment, William III and his government were blamed.

William's attitude to Scotland justifies Fletcher of Saltoun's remark that Scotland was 'as a farm managed by servants and not under the eye of the master'. William III was not only King of Great Britain, he was a European ruler who dedicated his life to resisting the expansionist ambitions of Louis XIV. Scotland received a very small proportion of his attention, but

England too was of secondary importance to him. Unsurprisingly, he was not popular in either kingdom, though in England, without Glencoe or Darien to discolour his memory, his reputation stands higher. William died in 1702, having been predeceased by Mary in 1694. William had recognized the danger to Anglo-Scottish relations which had been caused by conflicting commercial interests, and in his mind there was an obvious solution. 'Nothing,' he said, shortly before he died, 'can contribute more to the present and future peace, security and happiness of England and Scotland, than a firm and entire union between them.'

From the viewpoint of England, union had been growing increasingly desirable since the Revolution. The abolition of the Lords of the Articles had given the Scottish Parliament a freedom of action which had made Scotland and England more separate than they had been since the Union of Crowns. The Darien episode had illustrated what unhappy consequences could result when independent parliaments co-existed under a regal union. The early years of the next reign witnessed increasing enmity, to which, paradoxically, an 'entire union' seemed to offer the best solution.

William III, whose marriage had been childless, was succeeded by his sister-in-law, the last Stuart sovereign, Queen Anne. It was Anne's tragedy that though she bore many children to her husband, Prince George of Denmark, none survived infancy except a son, William, Duke of Gloucester, who died at the age of eleven in 1700. Since the son of James VII and II was being brought up as a Catholic in France, the English Parliament passed an Act of Settlement in 1701, which declared that the Crown should pass to the nearest

Protestant heiress, Sophia, Electress of Hanover (the daughter of Elizabeth of Bohemia, and granddaughter of James VI and I), and to her descendants. Scotland did not automatically follow England's example. As the Scots were still debarred from participation in England's overseas trade, the Scottish Parliament took the opportunity of showing its resentment by refusing to agree to the English Act of Settlement. Queen Anne's first Parliament, aware of the possibility that Scotland might accept the Jacobite succession and receive the support of Louis XIV, appointed commissioners to discuss terms of union; but the move was premature, and these negotiations came to nothing.

The Scottish Parliament which met in 1703, though it proved to be the last before the Union, showed a strongly independent spirit. It passed the Act anent Peace and War, which asserted the necessity of Scotland's consent to either, and the Wine Act, which declared Scotland's right to continue the wine trade with France while England and France were at war. The next year it passed the Act of Security, by which Scotland repudiated the Hanoverian succession, except upon terms which secured Scotland's Crown, Parliament, religion and trade against English control. This Act, which came close to being a full assertion of Scottish independence, and contained an implicit threat to sever the regal union, provoked the English Parliament to retaliate with the Alien Act, which required Scotland to accept the Hanoverian succession by Christmas Day 1705, otherwise Scots would be regarded as foreigners, debarred from trade with England and subjected to various legal disabilities (thereby losing the privileges which James VI and I had gained for the *post-nati*). Under these circumstances, which contained elements of coercion by the country which possessed the commercial advantage, the Union was accepted as a necessity. Commissioners for both kingdoms were appointed, and the Treaty of Union was drafted during 1706.

The Union deprived Scotland of the status of a separate nation; Great Britain, a familiar name since 1603, became a definitive term. To the new Parliament of Great Britain, Scotland sent forty-five commons to join an existing five hundred and thirteen, while sixteen Scottish peers joined an upper house of one hundred and ninety. In recompense for assuming a share in England's National Debt, Scotland received an 'Equivalent' of £398,085.10s., and the Scots were admitted to equal trading rights at home and abroad. The English coinage superseded that of Scotland, and the English customs and excise laws (with various temporary exemptions) became applicable in Scotland. It was agreed that the religion and the legal system of Scotland should remain unaltered.

On 25 March 1707 the Scottish Parliament met for the last time, and concluded its final transactions. At the end of the session the Earl of Seafield, Lord Privy Seal, remarked in famous words: 'There's the end of an auld sang.' Though the Union was officially complete from 1 May 1707, his frequently quoted saying was more epigrammatic than accurate.

CHAPTER SEVEN

Old Loyalties
1707 – 1745

The Union had been negotiated by nominated Commissioners, and it had been fiercely debated in the Scottish Parliament. The populace of Scotland had not been consulted. Although in theory the commons were represented in Parliament the franchise was so narrow that the spectrum of opinion represented was extremely small. The Edinburgh mob had been able to show its opinion during the pre-Union debate only by cheering those who were believed to oppose the Union and stoning those who were believed to support it. From all parts of the country Parliament received anti-Union petitions, which, in the opinion of the Duke of Argyll, were fit only to 'makes kites'. In these circumstances the Union was generally detested, as Daniel Defoe recognized when he visited Scotland shortly after it had taken place. 'I never saw a nation so universally wild,' he wrote, '. . . it seems a perfect gangrene of the temper.'

To people who had no understanding of the concept of a National Debt, the payment of the 'Equivalent' to Scotland looked suspiciously like a bribe, which had persuaded the pro-Unionists to sell the independence of Scotland to England. When the 'Equivalent' reached Edinburgh, in twelve wagons of bullion guarded by a detachment of 120 dragoons, the mob stoned the escort for bringing the price of Scotland's freedom. A

Jacobite song proclaimed 'We are bought and sold for English gold,' a statement which was widely believed. Though this view oversimplified the situation, it revealed a basic recognition that commercial interests had played a great part in the making of the Union.

By the Union of Parliaments the Scottish Nation lost its political identity. In principle, the Union was to have been a merger, whereby both Scotland and England were to have lost their identities, in order to become the United Kingdom. But the fact that the two parliaments were merged in the Westminster Parliament made it obvious that the English Parliament had absorbed that of Scotland, a fact which was emphasized by the small number of Scottish lords and commons who journeyed to Westminster. Neither the English nor the Scots showed any willingness to relinquish their national identities in a voluntary merger, but while the identity of the English was in no danger of being submerged, that of the Scots was immediately put on the defensive.

After the Union the national identity was most obviously embodied in those institutions which the Treaty of Union had acknowledged as inviolably Scottish: the Presbyterian Church and the Scottish Law. It was not long before the autonomy of both was threatened. The first incident which revealed how ill protected were these Scottish institutions by the terms of the Union was the prosecution of an Episcopalian clergyman, the Reverend James Greenshields, for using the Book of Common Prayer. Greenshields, sentenced by the Court of Session, appealed to the House of Lords. Since the peerages of Scotland and England had been merged in the Peerage of Great Britain, it was implicit in the terms of the

Union that the House of Lords must be the ultimate Court of Appeal, but it was one in which acquaintance with Scottish Law was inevitably scanty. The negotiators of the Union either had not thought of this, or had trusted that no test case would rapidly be brought. The House of Lords angered Presbyterian opinion by finding in favour of Greenshields. Following this decision, Parliament passed a Toleration Act in favour of Episcopalians (provided they abjured Jacobitism), which may have been praiseworthy in itself but undoubtedly contravened the terms of the Union.

In 1712 Parliament passed the Patronage Act, which restored the rights of lairds to appoint ministers to churches situated on their properties. By this Act the pre-Revolutionary patronage controversy was revived in all its bitterness to plague the Church of Scotland continuously until patronage was finally abolished by Disraeli's government in 1874. The extension of the Malt Tax to Scotland in 1713 also caused widespread resentment, not only because it too contravened the terms of the Union but because it had the effect of raising the price of ale, which suggested to ordinary people that they were paying for the Union through their most basic pleasures. A Scottish member's protest in Parliament brought forth an English member's rejoinder: 'Have we not bought the Scots, and a right to tax them?'

Unsurprisingly, some Scots who had been enthusiastic to negotiate the Union had second thoughts. In 1713 the Duke of Argyll and the Earl of Seafield, both of whom had been ardently pro-Union, moved the repeal of the Union in the House of Lords. The motion was defeated by four proxy votes. By the decision of this small, absentee majority the United Kingdom continued its existence. Thenceforward the identity of Scotland was dependent for its survival upon the separate character of Scottish culture; a cultural identity is more difficult to define than a political identity, and consequently more difficult to defend.

Widespread distaste for the Union did much to revive the hopes of the Jacobites. When James VII and II died in France in 1701, Louis XIV immediately acknowledged his thirteen-year-old son as James VIII of Scotland and III of England. With this encouragement the Jacobites placed great reliance on the prospect of French help in re-establishing the legitimate Stuart succession. The unpopularity of the Union offered the first promising opportunity for the attempt to be made.

Prince James Edward Stuart was an intelligent but austere young man who won the respect of those who knew him well but lacked the inspirational qualities required to revive a fading cause. His first attempt to regain his kingdoms was made in 1708, when a French fleet brought him within sight of the Scottish coast. An encounter with English warships and a violent storm deterred the French commander from attempting a landing, and despite the vehement opposition of James himself, the fleet sailed back to France. The best Jacobite opportunity to win general support in Scot-land, when anti Union feeling was at its height, was thus thrown away.

James Edward, on his return to France, sought the military experience which he needed by serving incognito in the French army. He distinguished himself at the Battles of Oudenarde and Malplaquet, but it was no help to his cause that he was fighting against the English, whom he regarded as his natural subjects. In 1713, with the cessation of Anglo-French hostilities, Louis XIV was obliged by the Treaty of Utrecht to recognize the Hanoverian succession and abandon his patronage of 'the Pretender'. James Edward tactfully withdrew from French territory before Louis was obliged to expel him, but thenceforward his greatest difficulty in plotting his restoration was the problem of communications, as was shortly revealed.

On the death of Queen Anne in 1714, James Edward might have gained his kingdoms by conversion to Protestantism, but he refused to compromise his convictions. Nonetheless, he was no Catholic bigot like his father. Some years later he wrote 'I am a Catholic, but I am a King, and subjects of whatever religion they may be, have an equal right to be protected, I am a King, but ... I am not an apostle. I am not bound to convert my people otherwise than by my example, nor to show apparent partiality to Catholics, which would only serve to injure them later.' Such a sane approach to the conflicting demands of personal and state religion might have saved the throne of James VII and II, but it could not serve to reverse the Act of Settlement in favour of his son. Queen Anne had been predeceased by the Electress of Hanover, whose son, under the terms of the Act, became King George I of Great Britain.

The Jacobite Rising of 1715 was intended to take advantage of the personal unpopularity of George I, but it was essentially too late, in that it took place against a King who had had time to become established. The Rising was led by John Erskine, sixth Earl

of Mar, who had been one of the signatories of the
Treaty of Union, but had become disillusioned with its
results, and dissatisfied with his own rewards. On 26
August Mar held a *tinchal*, or hunting party, in
Braemar, a great sporting occasion which provided a
pretext for a gathering of armed men, and sufficiently
concealed a warlike meeting of Jacobites. Mar was at
least a good orator. On 6 September he raised the
Royal Standard and proclaimed King James VIII and
III, making a bid for popular support in a speech
denouncing the Union. The response was impressive.
Mar rapidly gathered an army of 5000 Highlanders
with which, on 16 September, he captured Perth. This
success encouraged further support, and his army grew
until it reached 12,000. But, instead of making use of
his victory to take Stirling and if possible Edinburgh,
Mar made the fatal decision to remain at Perth to await
the arrival of James Edward.

A force of 2000 Jacobites under the more enterpris-
ing MacIntosh of Borlum attempted to surprise
Edinburgh, but was successfully prevented by the
Duke of Argyll, who commanded the Government
troops. Argyll's moves to repeal the Union had been
purely political, and he had no interest in associating
himself with activities which the Government could
only regard as treasonable. Support of the Government at this juncture gave him the means to increase
his personal power in Scotland. MacIntosh of Borlum,
abandoning his attempt on Edinburgh, sought support
for the Rising in England, was forced by Jacobites from
the south-west of Scotland led by Lord Kenmure,
by a force of English Jacobites under Lord Derwentwater. They invaded England by the western route,
only to be defeated at Preston on 14 November.

In the meantime the forces of Mar and Argyll had met in battle at Sheriffmuir, near Dunblane. Tactically the battle was indecisive, as a well-known verse amusingly conveys:

> Sum say that we wan
> An' sum say that they wan,
> An' sum say that nane wan at a', man;
> But o' ane thing I'm sure,
> That at Sheriffmuir
> A battle there was, which I saw, man...

But strategically the advantage lay with Argyll, since if the Rising were to succeed it needed to succeed quickly; in fact, it failed, and failed slowly.

Poor communications had left James Edward uninformed of Mar's activities until a late stage. His difficulties in crossing France in secrecy prevented his reaching Scotland until 22 December, when he landed at Peterhead. His sojourn in Scotland was brief and disappointing. The intention of his supporters had been to crown him at Scone, but though he came as far south as Perth, desertions from Mar's army and the advance of Argyll put an end to the enterprise. Early in February 1716 James Edward left Scotland, accompanied by Mar, and their remaining supporters scattered, to save themselves as best they could.

Despite the failure of the '15 James Edward did not relinquish his hopes of restoration. Promises of Spanish support led him to visit Spain in the spring of 1719. The result of his mission was a small-scale Spanish invasion of Scotland, which was supported by Scottish Jacobites led by the Earl Marischal; but the combined force met defeat in Glenshiel, in June. For some time James Edward's marriage had been under negotiation, and while he was in Spain he was married by proxy to a Polish princess, Maria Clementina Sobieska. In the autumn of 1719 he settled with her in Rome, where the Jacobite court became a centre of intrigue and espionage. Clementina bore her husband two sons: Charles Edward, born in 1720, and Henry Benedict, born in 1725. The elder, whose adventurous early life was to create the legend of 'Bonnie Prince Charlie', was brought up with an almost messianic sense of destiny. From early childhood he accepted that his mission was to regain Great Britain for his father and the succession for his family. Many years later he had a medal struck which bore his profile, and on the reverse the legend *Amor et Spes Britanniae* ('the Love and Hope of Britain'): such was the image of himself with which he grew up.

In the meantime, Scotland experienced the aftermath of the alarm which resurgent Jacobitism had caused the Government. Lords Kenmure and Derwentwater, captured at Preston, were executed, and the Government ordered the disarming of the clans. This was a measure which failed in its objective, since those clans which had supported the Government surrendered their weapons, while the Jacobite clans surrendered obsolete firearms and outworn swords, keeping their best weapons to fight again another day. Significantly, they had no doubt that the day would come.

A more effective method of making the Highlands amenable to Government control was the improvement of communications. In 1726, General Wade, who had been responsible for implementing the Disarming Act, was entrusted with the construction of a system of military roads, to link Fort George, Fort Augustus,* Fort William, Inverness and Crieff. The result of ten years' work was 260 miles of roads, and over thirty bridges. This great enterprise was the first breach in the immemorial isolation of the Highlands. The original purpose of Wade's roads was to facilitate the movement of troops policing the Highlands, but in more peaceful times they were used by ordinary travellers, who were reminded of their debt of gratitude by a doggerel inscription near Fort William:

Had you seen these roads before they were made
You would hold up your hands and bless General
Wade.

The accession of George II in 1727 was unmarked by Jacobite disturbances, for James Edward had abandoned active attempts at restoration, and Charles Edward was still a small child. George II, however, was no more popular than his father, nor did his all-powerful minister Sir Robert Walpole endear his regime to the Scots by increased taxation on wine, brandy and tea. The consequence was an increase in smuggling, encouraged by popular adulation of smugglers as anti-Government heroes. In 1736, this situation caused a sensational outbreak of disorder, when Captain Porteous of the City Guard ordered his men to fire on an Edinburgh crowd which was protesting at a smuggler's execution. Porteous was sentenced to death in Scotland, but reprieved by the Queen,

*At this period Fort Augustus was called Kilcumin. It was renamed in honour of William Augustus, Duke of Cumberland, whose claims to fame are mentioned later in this chapter.

Caroline of Ansbach, who was acting as Regent in George II's absence. Following his reprieve, Porteous was removed from prison and lynched during the night, by 'persons unknown'. The Government responded by passing a Bill of Pains and Penalties, under which the City Charter of Edinburgh was to be destroyed, the City Guard disbanded, the Netherbow Port demolished and the Provost imprisoned. These penalties were commuted to a fine, through the intervention of the Duke of Argyll and Duncan Forbes of Culloden, the Lord President of the Court of Session, whose great influence with the Government was consistently exerted in favour of his countrymen. The 'Porteous Riot' had no Jacobite significance, but it could not fail to encourage the Jacobites, as evidence of the Government's unpopularity.

In England, Tory resentment of Walpole's Whig ministry led to an upsurge of sentimental Jacobitism. The Jacobite cause inspired an extraordinary outburst of lyricism, which afforded the disaffected the satisfying outlet of singing Jacobite songs, and drinking the health of 'the King over the Water'. In the Highlands of Scotland Jacobitism remained a cause to be fought for, but of the English Jacobites a contemporary cynically remarked that 'no people in the Universe knew better the difference between drinking and fighting.' This decisive distinction was illustrated by the events of the last Jacobite Rising, which occurred when foreign affairs briefly favoured the cause and Prince Charles Edward Stuart reached maturity.

In 1740 the death of the Emperor Charles VI and the accession of Maria Theresa precipitated the War of the Austrian Succession. A great European convulsion offered Prince Charles Edward the chance for which his whole life had been a preparation. As in 1715 Jacobite hopes centred on French assistance, while the French Government prepared to make use of the exiled Stuarts in the interests of France. The plan which took shape in 1743 was far from chimerical. Charles Edward was to land in England with 10,000 French troops, adequately supplied with French arms and money; and on these conditions the Scottish Jacobite chiefs engaged to match the French force with an equally large army of Highlanders. One of the leading Gaelic poets of the day, Alasdair mac Mhaighstir Alasdair, anticipated the Prince's coming in stirring verse:

> With eastern winds will come o'er seas
>   One we've keenly hoped for,
> With many men and shining arms,
>   Ready, quick, unhindered;
> Prince Charles Stuart, the son of James,
>   The Crown's heir from his exile.
> Let every Briton homage do
>   On bended knees before him.*

Charles Edward left Rome in a spirit of high optimism, taking leave of his father with the words, 'I go, Sire, in search of three Crowns, which I doubt not but to have the honour of laying at your Majesty's feet.' He crossed France in disguise, to join the expedition which was assembling at Dunkirk, under the command of the Maréchal de Saxe. In January 1744 disaster struck the expedition, when the transport ships were destroyed by storms. Initially, Charles Edward hoped that this would prove to be a mere

*trans. John Lorne Campbell.

setback, but time passed and it became increasingly obvious that the invasion plan had been shelved. When 1745 opened with a French victory over combined English and Dutch forces at Fontenoy, a Jacobite Rising against the English Government ceased to be of interest to France.

Charles Edward was disappointed but undaunted; he was determined not to return to Rome with reports of failure. 'If it is impossible to transport the necessary troops to England,' he wrote to his father, 'the best will be to turn our thoughts to Scotland.' The Jacobite Rising of 1745 originated in the Prince's determination to fulfil the purpose to which his upbringing had been dedicated, and in his conviction that Scottish and English Jacobites only awaited his arrival to rise as one man and hail him as 'the Love and Hope of Britain'. Songs, toasts and the over-sanguine reports of Jacobite agents combined to fuel his magnificent misapprehension.

The Prince did not inform his father of his audacious decision to sail to Scotland, alone if necessary, until it was too late for James to stop him. He left France on 5 July 1745 with two ships, one of which was intercepted by an English warship and forced to return. Charles Edward continued, and on 23 July he landed on Eriskay in the Outer Hebrides with his handful of companions, 'the Seven Men of Moidart'. The extraordinary legend of 'Bonnie Prince Charlie' had begun. (The origin of this nickname, which the purists avoid as a vulgarism, is in fact the Gaelic form of the Prince's name *Tearlach* which can be heard in a transitional form in the Jacobite song 'You're welcome, Charlie Stuart'.)

Charles Edward was not very welcome on his arrival

in Scotland. The chiefs were unwilling to raise their clansmen without the promised French support; memories of the end of the '15 very reasonably made them hesitant. MacDonald of Boisdale advised the Prince to 'go home', to which Charles Edward replied, 'I am come home, Sir, and will entertain no notion at all of returning to that place from whence I came, for I am persuaded my faithful Highlanders will stand by me.' Charles Edward was always capable of a dramatic turn of phrase, and he possessed an instinctive sense of the moment at which an appeal to the emotions would draw men to his cause. The early success of the '45 owed much to his optimistic fervour, which contrasted so remarkably with his father's fatalism. Whereas James Edward's lack of leadership had allowed an army to disperse, Charles Edward's charismatic qualities drew an army into existence.

MacDonald of Clanranald and Cameron of Lochiel brought the Prince a force of about nine hundred clansmen. On 19 August he raised his standard in Glenfinnan at the head of Lochshiel, and proclaimed his father King James VIII and III. He then marched towards the Lowlands, making use of General Wade's road over the Pass of Corrieyairack. The Jacobite army grew by the way, and easily captured Perth, where the Prince was joined by Lord George Murray, brother of the Duke of Atholl, whose military experience compensated for his own lack of it. On 17 September Charles Edward entered Edinburgh, and once again proclaimed his father, at the Mercat Cross. Though he failed to capture the Castle he rode in triumph to Holyrood, where he held his court during the ensuing weeks.

Charles Edward gained his most impressive victory

on 21 September, over an English force commanded by Sir John Cope, at the Battle of Prestonpans, just south of Edinburgh. This battle was the high point of his success, after which he delayed too long in Edinburgh, in the hope of receiving reinforcements from France. Arms and money were sent him, but not the additional soldiers which he needed. He swiftly became convinced that if his gains in Scotland were not followed by an invasion of England, they would be as swiftly lost, especially as Wade had by this time arrived at Newcastle, where he was only awaiting certain reinforcements before invading Scotland.

Accordingly, though the Jacobite army had won few recruits in the Lowlands, and had reached a total of only about eight thousand, Charles Edward determined upon invasion. Early in November the Jacobite advance on London began. George II received the news with such terror that he was reported to be preparing to retire to Hanover. However, his son, William Augustus, Duke of Cumberland, was commissioned to raise a second army to take the field against the Prince.

The beginning of the advance into England was also the beginning of the Jacobite disillusionment. There was no massive rising in Charles Edward's favour. Three hundred recruits formed the 'Manchester Regiment', but apart from a few individuals no more had joined the Prince by the time that his army reached Derby on 4 December. One hundred and thirty miles from London, the Prince's officers lost their nerve. Headed by Lord George Murray, an able but cautious commander, they demanded that the Prince turn north again, to consolidate his gains in Scotland. Hitherto Charles Edward's success had been due to his incredible audacity, and it is just conceivable that audacity might have won London, though only massive reinforcements from France or a general Jacobite Rising could have maintained such a victory. Once audacity was called in question, the only possibility of victory was lost. Charles Edward's optimism ceased to inspire his officers in the face of lack of English support; it began to alarm them, and they demanded that military decisions be submitted to a Committee of Commanders. Charles Edward resisted, and was overruled; the committee was formed, and determined upon retreat.

The Jacobite army was back in Scotland by 20 December, and the northward march, organized by Lord George Murray, continued. In January 1746 the Prince won his last victory at Falkirk, routing a slightly larger force commanded by General Hawley. Charles Edward was eager to take advantage of this success by capturing Stirling Castle, but the siege showed little sign of quick success, and once again his officers urged him to withdraw further north. The Prince acquiesced sullenly, and withdrew to establish his headquarters at Inverness, where inactivity rapidly lowered the morale of his army. In the meantime, the Duke of Cumberland was assembling his troops at Aberdeen. In the knowledge that time was on his side, Cumberland ensured that his preparations should be thorough. His army was well provisioned, and that of the Prince was facing starvation, when the decisive battle was fought on 16 April, on Culloden Moor, near Inverness.

Culloden was the end of the Jacobite Rising, for Cumberland's expert artillery fire inflicted terrible slaughter upon the Highlanders. But Cumberland gained no glory by his victory, for the atrocities which his soldiers committed after the battle gained him the name of 'Butcher Cumberland'. Some of the wounded were shot or bayoneted as they lay on the field and others were burned alive; and when Duncan Forbes of Culloden interceded for humanitarian treatment of the vanquished he was insulted by Cumberland, who contemptuously referred to him as 'that old woman who spoke to me of humanity.'

Charles Edward survived the battle, and escaped one of the most famous manhunts in history. From April to September 1746, with a price of £30,000 on his head, he evaded capture, fleeing from the Scottish mainland to North and South Uist, to Skye, and back to the mainland again. Highlanders and Islanders contemptuously ignored a reward which represented almost untold wealth to them, and the Prince was helped on his way by many people besides the one most admired and best remembered, Flora MacDonald. At last, on 14 September, Charles Edward was taken on board the French brig *L'Heureux*, which had been sent in search of him, and he landed in France on 1 October.

Initially, Charles Edward did not recognize his defeat as final. He returned to France apparently in the expectation that he had only to reappear in person to demand the help of Louis XV in order to receive it. Disillusionment came to him painfully and slowly, as he came to realize that heroic failure might be admired and pitied, but help would be given only for political reasons, which no longer existed. The remainder of Charles Edward's life, as a wandering exile, was a personal tragedy, but no longer a part of the history of Scotland. He died without legitimate issue, in 1788.*

The Jacobite Rising of 1745 was a political and military adventure inspired by the will of one man. It was not, as even some English contemporaries imagined, a 'Scotch rebellion' against England; there were more Scots in the Government armies than in the army of the Prince. For this reason the '45 had something of the character of a Scottish Civil War, but it was not a war between the Highlands and the Lowlands, for some clans, including the Campbells, Mackays, Munros, Macleods, and Grants supported the Government, while others, the MacDonalds, MacPhersons and Frasers among them, were divided. In some ways the '45 can be seen as a prolongation of the religious strife of the previous century, since recent research has shown that approximately 70 per cent of the Prince's supporters were Catholics and 30 per cent Episcopalians. The Presbyterian Lowlanders had no desire to risk a return to the religious policies of Charles II and James VII, and would not put their trust in the promised toleration of the latter's Catholic son and grandson.

Considering how narrowly based was the support given to Charles Edward, the defeat of the '45 appears inevitable, yet inevitability is a concept of which historians have learned to be wary. Recently an eminent Scottish historian has written: 'It would be rash to dismiss the '45 as Celtic moonshine ... It had no such appearance in 1745, not to the Government, to the rebels, to the general public ...' Indeed, the

---

*His younger brother, Prince Henry Benedict, entered the Church of Rome, and became a Cardinal. Before his death, in 1807, he acknowledged King George III as the legitimate heir of the Stuarts.

atrocities committed upon the vanquished, and the reprisals later inflicted on the Highlands, were the measure of the fear which the last Jacobite Rising had caused.

CHAPTER EIGHT

North Britain
1745 – 1850

In Scotland as a whole, by 1745, the Union was accepted. In the thirty-eight years which had passed since it was negotiated a new generation had grown up, to which the Union was an historical event. The promises made by James Edward and Charles Edward Stuart to restore Scotland to its 'ancient, free and independent' condition were shown to be less alluring, particularly in the Lowlands, than the advantages of the existing situation. By 1745 the Lowlands had begun to enjoy a new economic prosperity which appeared to be a direct consequence of the Union. When the excitement engendered by preparation for the unhappy Darien venture had led Fletcher of Saltoun to observe of his countrymen that 'by an unforeseen change in the genius of the nation, all their thoughts and inclinations seemed to be turned upon trade', he had probably observed a natural revulsion against the religious strife of the seventeenth century; but after the Union, that 'unforeseen change', if such it had been, had found certain outlets previously denied to it. As a result of the Union, the Scots were admitted to trade with the American colonies; and the west coast ports, especially Glasgow, rapidly entered a period of unexampled prosperity.

In 1718 the first Glasgow-owned ship crossed the Atlantic, the harbinger of the establishment of Glasgow as the centre of the Scottish tobacco trade. Tobacco was shipped to Glasgow for re-import to Europe because the American colonies were forbidden by the British Government to trade directly with Europe. Besides tobacco, the American colonists exported rum and sugar to Scotland, and Scottish merchants supplied them with manufactured goods which they were as yet unable to produce for themselves.

Scottish linen was especially in demand in America, and the diverse processes of linen production – preparation of the flax, spinning, weaving, bleaching and dyeing – were carried out as a home industry throughout most of Scotland. The Board of Trustees for Manufactures, founded in 1727, encouraged the industry by offering prizes for good workmanship and by providing capital. Both commercial and manufacturing aspects of the industry were also assisted by the development of banking. The Bank of Scotland had been founded in 1695, and it was followed by the Royal Bank of Scotland in 1727 and the British Linen Bank in 1746.

The tobacco trade slumped with the American War of Independence (1775–83), and after the war it failed to recover, because the Americans were able to establish their own direct trade with Europe. Thereafter the Glasgow merchants invested their fortunes in the cotton industry. The linen industry declined slowly, but cotton spinning did not take its place as a home industry, for the mechanization of production through the invention of Hargreaves's spinning jenny and Arkwright's water frame led to the establishment of cotton mills where there was water-power available – the first at Rothesay in 1779. Most of the cotton mills were founded in Renfrewshire and Lanarkshire. By 1795 the great pioneer industrialist David Dale had established four mills at New Lanark, in which he employed 1334 workers. In 1799 Dale's son-in-law, Robert Owen, took over the management of the New Lanark Mills, and attempted to provide education and decent working conditions for the child-workers who were the most tragic victims of the Industrial Revolution.

The second half of the eighteenth century was a fertile age of invention in which Scottish genius was particularly prominent. James Watt patented the steam engine in 1769, and it was gradually applied to a great variety of industries. Early in the next century two Scots pioneered steam navigation. In 1802 William Symington built the steam paddle tug *Charlotte Dundas*, which towed barges through the Forth-Clyde Canal (which had been opened in 1790); and in 1811 Henry Bell built the *Comet*, a sail-assisted steam-ship, which plied between Glasgow and Greenock, with a library of classical literature on board to divert those passengers who required more to interest them than the pleasure of the voyage and the novelty of the transport!

By 1823 seventy-two steamers had been built on the Clyde, and twenty-three in other Scottish shipyards. From Leith, in 1838, came the *Sirius*, the first ship to cross the Atlantic under steam (using 450 tons of coal to do so). At the same time, Scotland was building the last commercial sailing ships, the tea-clippers, whose racing voyages to the Far East brought the age of sail to its end in drama and beauty. The famous *Thermopylae* was launched from Aberdeen in 1868, and the even more famous *Cutty Sark* from Dumbarton the following year. She was named after the young witch in Burns's poem *Tam O' Shanter*, who wore a 'cutty sark' or short shift, as does the female figurehead of the ship.

From the 1830s onwards, iron began to be used in shipbuilding, giving further encouragement to an already well-established Scottish industry. The first iron-foundries in Scotland dated from the 1720s, when they had been set up by English iron-masters who leased large tracts of Scottish forest to supply the necessary timber. To furnaces at Invergarry, Taynuilt and Inveraray the iron ore was brought to the fuel at vast expense. Abram Darby's discovery of the use of coke for iron-smelting in 1750 enabled furnaces to be constructed near existing coalfields, with the added advantage that coal and iron ore were frequently to be found in the same neighbourhoods.

The first Scottish foundry to use coke was the Carron Iron Works, established near Falkirk in 1759. It served the arts of war and peace by the manufacture of both armaments and agricultural machinery. Some of the guns of Nelson's *Victory* were cast in the Carron foundries, as were the field-guns used by Wellington in the Peninsular War. While iron was in demand for armaments during the Napoleonic Wars, the need for it continued to increase in peacetime. In 1828 the invention of the 'hot blast' process by James Neilson reduced the cost of production by a 75 per cent reduction in the tonnage of coal needed to produce each ton of iron. More and more ironworks were opened, as a result of the discovery of blackband ironstone in the district of Monkland, Lanarkshire. From the 20,000 tons of pig-iron annually produced during the Napoleonic Wars, by 1857, the total

Scottish output of iron was two and a half million tons.

This enormous increase of iron production led to an accompanying expansion of coalmining. Coal had been used as fuel in Scotland since the Middle Ages. When Aeneas Sylvius Piccolomini – the future Pope Pius II – had visited Scotland as a Papal envoy in the reign of James I, he had been astonished to see 'black stones' handed to beggars at the church doors. This had been a more practical form of charity than he had recognized! In 1617 James VI had visited the coalmine at Culross, which was reputed to extend a mile under the Firth of Forth. But most seventeenth- and eighteenth-century mining was either surface-mining or mining in shallow pits, for in most places the problem of drainage remained insurmountable. By an extraordinary legal anachronism Scottish miners remained in a condition of serfdom – 'thirled' to their labour, to use the Scots expression – until legislation of 1799 gave them the freedom which other Scottish labouring men had enjoyed since at least the time of the Wars of Independence. However, in the many new coalmines which were opened in Ayrshire, Lanarkshire, Fife and Lothian during the first half of the nineteenth century it may be doubted whether the miners' freedom was much more than theoretical. The economic enslavement of long hours and low wages was the lot of men who were obliged to accept any conditions of employment which were available as the only alternative to starvation. In consequence, in any family as many members as possible would seek work; and many women and children were employed as hauliers in the mines, before the Mines Act of 1842 forbade their employment underground.

While the first phase of the Industrial Revolution began to transform the counties of the Forth-Clyde area of Scotland into an industrial belt, a slower but no less effective change had been taking place throughout the Lowlands. The Agrarian Revolution had begun before the Union, and it continued throughout the eighteenth century and into the nineteenth. With the restoration of peaceful conditions in the last years of the seventeenth century there was every reason for Lowland landowners to feel that efforts at agricultural improvement might be permitted to continue undisturbed. At the same time, from 1696 onwards there were seven lean years of summer rainstorms and early winters, which made improvement not only desirable but absolutely necessary.

The traditional method of Scottish farming, practised since the Middle Ages, was known as the 'run-rig' system. After the Reformation the monastic lands, once farmed efficiently by the monks, especially those of the Cistercian Order, fell into the hands of the 'Lords of Erection' and the Protestant lairds who at the time had little interest in agriculture, so that the methods of the monks were forgotten, and the more primitive ways used on the secular estates of medieval Scotland had taken their place. A group of tenants inhabiting a village or 'ferm-toun' would have a series or 'run' of strips of land known as 'rigs' allotted to them. There would be an 'in-field' and an 'out-field'. The in-field would be manured and sown with oats or barley year after year; the out-field would never be fertilized, but would be sown until the soil it exhausted, and then abandoned for some years, until it became capable of production again.

A number of Scottish landowners recognized the

need to revolutionize a method of farming which had become ineffective to support the population. The first to contribute to a topical branch of literature was James Donaldson, who published *Husbandry Anatomized* in 1697. Donaldson suggested that the rigs should be enclosed, so that each tenant had a compact area to farm; and he urged more fertilization, the rotation of crops, and the cultivation of potatoes. In 1699 Lord Belhaven wrote the *Countryman's Diary*, and MacIntosh of Borlum, in prison for his Jacobite activities, wrote a treatise on agriculture. An English book which recommended hoeing and turnip growing, Jethro Tull's *Horse-Hoeing Husbandry*, published in 1733, was eagerly read in Scotland; and Lord Kames, a Scottish judge and philosopher, who owned great estates in Berwickshire, published *The Gentleman Farmer* in 1776, which ran into several editions.

One of the most famous of the Scottish agricultural improvers was Sir Archibald Grant, whose father, Lord Cullen, presented him with the estate of Monymusk on his marriage in 1717. The estate was in poor condition, but Sir Archibald regarded it as a challenge. He enclosed and drained his land, planted turnips, introduced crop rotation, and was successful in growing wheat, which had previously been little known in Scotland, because the traditional farming methods had exhausted the land too much for it to grow. Sir Archibald Grant's fame as an agricultural improver was amusingly immortalized through another of his interests – choral music. A more liberal attitude to religion in the mid-eighteenth century permitted singing in church, and Sir Archibald held choir practices in his library, to the accompaniment of a chamber organ. At that period it was considered

improper to sing sacred words at rehearsal, and so
secular verses were composed for the purpose. One of
them, substituting the dwelling-place of the laird for
the Lord, proclaimed:

> How lovely is thy dwelling-place
> Sir Archie Grant, to me;
> The home-park and the policies,
> How pleasant, Sir, they be.

No doubt they were very pleasant indeed, for Sir
Archie Grant planted many trees on his land, and his
tree-nurseries produced over a million saplings for
transplantation, a valuable contribution to reafforesta-
tion at a time when industry was burning Scottish
forests away.

The inventive spirit of the Industrial Revolution,
however, made its own contribution to the improvement of agriculture. In 1764 James Small of Dalkeith
invented the 'swing-plough' with a metal ploughshare,
which could be worked by one man with two horses
– a wonderful improvement on the old wooden plough
which required a team of eight or ten oxen, steered,
encouraged and belaboured by several men and
women. The threshing machine, invented by Andrew
Meikle of Dunbar in 1784, was at first received with
suspicion, and regarded by some traditionally-minded
farmers as an invention of the Devil; but gradually its
labour-saving capacity overcame prejudice. Agricultural machinery received something like a guarantee of
non-Diabolical origin early in the nineteenth century,
when the Reverend Patrick Bell invented the mechani-
cal reaper. With the outbreak of the Napoleonic Wars,
agricultural improvements and the mechanization of

farming both contributed to the increased prosperity of the Lowlands, for more home-produced food was needed, and the Lowland farmers were able to provide it.

The developments in trade, industry and agriculture which changed the face of Lowland Scotland during the course of the eighteenth century had little effect beyond the Highland Line. The changes which took place in the Highlands were principally social, and were almost universally unfortunate. Changes in Lowland society, rather than benefiting the Highlands, seemed to threaten the immemorial patterns of Highland life, and this is a contributory reason why Jacobitism appealed at least to some of the Highland clans, whereas to almost all Lowlanders it appeared to be anachronistic and irrelevant.

The consequences of the '45 seemed to be directly disastrous to the Highlands, yet those consequences did no more than accelerate a train of events which was already taking place. The general pacification of Scotland which followed the 1688 Revolution had already begun to make the military *raison d'être* of the clans anachronistic before the '15. Though the Disarming Act which followed the '15 was ineffective, the second Disarming Act of 1746 was far more vigorously enforced; and it was enforced alike on the Jacobite clans and on the clans which had been loyal to the Government. The disarming of the Highlands was not a short-term expedient to meet a political crisis: it had an ultimately transforming effect upon a traditionally militaristic society.

After the '45 Highland dress was also made illegal. In the words of the Dress Act every man or boy was forbidden 'to wear or put on the clothes commonly called Highland clothes, that is to say, the plaid, philabeg or little kilt, trowse, shoulder belt or any part whatsoever of what peculiarly belongs to the Highland garb; and that no tartan or party-coloured plaid or stuff shall be used for great-coats or for upper-coats'. The playing of the pipes was also forbidden, because the Duke of Cumberland had correctly observed that they were 'an instrument of war'. The proscription of Highland dress and Highland music was obviously intended as a measure destructive to the Gaelic way of life, which was seen to have fostered the strongest support for the Jacobite Risings. But other specifically economic measures did more to metamorphose the Highlands, without integrating them with Lowland Scotland.

In 1746 the Heritable Jurisdictions of the Highland chiefs were abolished (a measure which James VI had recommended in *Basilikon Doron*, as a means of enhancing the power of the central government, but which he had lacked the strength to introduce). The rule of the chiefs had been at best paternalistic, at worst tyrannical, and it is romanticism to suppose that the best had been consistently representative. But the demilitarization of the Highlands and the abolition of the Heritable Jurisdictions had the effect of turning the chiefs into landlords. Until these changes had taken place, a chief had been concerned to maintain the largest possible number of potential fighting men on his lands, to keep up the strength of the clan as a military unit capable of defending itself against powerful neighbours – whose motives were, of course, exactly the same. A chief would grant a 'tack' or lease to a 'tacksman', who was probably a cadet of his family, and the tacksman would sublet smaller parcels of land to as many tenants as the land would support. In time of war – such as the '45 itself – the tacksman would be the officer and the tenants would provide the rank and file of a Highland army. This type of organization became increasingly obsolete as the eighteenth century advanced, but the defeat of the '45 was its deathblow.

By an Act of 1752 forty Jacobite estates were forfeited, and for the next thirty years they were administered by Crown Commissioners. The Commissioners granted leases to tenants who were forbidden to sublet, so that a new class of tacksman could not emerge. In 1784 the forfeited estates were restored to the heirs of the former chiefs, but in the intervening time the old relationships between chiefs and clansmen had broken down. The restored chiefs, with a few exceptions, saw themselves merely as landed proprietors, and were principally interested in making a profit from their enormous tracts of land. In some instances they had an urgent need to repair their own shattered fortunes. A large population of fighting men had been necessary to the chiefs of warlike clans; a large population of people struggling to subsist on inhospitable land was unwelcome to the chiefs of the new dispensation. This problem was not one which faced Jacobite clans alone. Demilitarization had also left pro-Government chiefs with a surplus population of unwanted tenants. The necessity of making Highland estates profitable was one which cut across political affiliations. Landowners found a solution to their own problem in turning over their estates from cattle to sheep farming, but as an historian of the period has aptly remarked, 'the advance of sheep always involves the retreat of men', and on many estates whole families were evicted to make way for a few shepherds.

An easy way of removing tenants was to drive them from the land by raising their rents. As early as 1771, Thomas Pennant, in *A Tour of Scotland*, wrote of the Highlands:

> The rage of raising rents has reached this distant country ... Here the great men begin at the wrong end with squeezing the bag before they have helped the poor tenant to fill it by the introduction of manufactures ... numbers of families have been obliged to give up the strong attachment the Scots in general have for their country and exchange it for the wilds of America.

The unfortunate truth was that the 'great men' criticized by Pennant did not wish to help their tenants by introducing manufactures, they merely wished to clear their estates for sheep.

The most notorious of the 'Highland Clearances' were those carried out by the second Duke of Sutherland between 1811 and 1820, in which approximately 15,000 people were removed from the inland areas of the county, and forced to remake their lives on the coast. The Sutherland Clearances aroused intense bitterness, because the evictions of the tenants were carried out with needless brutality, which included burning the cottages of those who were reluctant to ... The Duke of Sutherland's intention was that the men transplanted to the coast, who had been miserably poor in their previous homes, should supplement their living by fishing, and by growing potatoes on the small crofts which were provided for them. They did not take kindly to the change, for the sea was unknown to them, and fishing was a dangerous skill, not quickly learned.

In the early years of the nineteenth century there was one coastal industry which assisted some of the crofters to earn a livelihood. Tons of seawrack were gathered and burned to make an alkaline ash, kelp, which was used as an agricultural fertilizer. The kelp industry prospered during the Napoleonic Wars, because of the difficulty of importing the more popular alkali made from barilla. At the height of the wartime boom kelp reached a price of £22 per ton, though the families which worked on producing it made only about £7 a year. The kelp industry was kept in existence after 1815 by a high import tax on barilla; but when the tax was removed in 1823, the price of kelp instantly fell. The families which had relied on the meagre supplement which it had provided faced destitution, and were forced to emigrate.

To those who remained, inured to hardship as they were, it must have seemed that the forces of nature grew increasingly inimical. The introduction of potatoes seemed to have provided a substantial and reliable supplement to the crofters' diet. But new misery came in 1846, when the Potato Blight which caused famine in Ireland reached Scotland also. Though its effects were not so terrible as in Ireland – where possibly 800,000 people died from starvation and the diseases which attended it – potatoes had come to form a sufficiently important part of the Highlanders' fare for the failure of the crop to cause widespread destitution, and to increase the number of emigrants to an unprecedented total of 106,000 in one year.

Many who did not emigrate looked for a better life

James Graham, Marquis of
Montrose, attributed to Honthorst.

John Graham of
Claverhouse, Viscount
Dundee, artist unknown

King James VII and II, an engraving by J. Smith after N. de Largillière

Prince James Edward Stuart, son of James VII and II (painting from Studio of Alexis Simeon Belle)

Prince Charles Edward Stuart, whose heroic attempt to make his father 'King James VIII and III' ended in defeat at Culloden (painting from Studio of A. David).

The philosopher David Hume, a leading figure of the Scottish Enlightenment, by Tassie

Robert Burns, Scotland's national poet, portrayed by Naismitt.

Dr Thomas Chalmers, who founded the Free Church of Scotland after the Disruption of 1843, by Thomas Duncan.

James Keir Hardie, founder of the Scottish Labour Party, by H. J. Dobson

Bust of the poet Hugh McDiarmid, leading spirit of the twentieth-century Scottish literary renaissance, by Benno Schotz.

in the industrial Lowlands, where for the most part, if they found subsistence, it was accompanied by new kinds of hardship: long hours (a fourteen-hour working day was normal); dangerous conditions of work in mines or factories; cramped and squalid living quarters in towns and cities which could not expand fast enough to accommodate growing populations in anything but insanitary overcrowding – a situation worsened by the fact that the care of public health was as yet a concept which belonged to the future.

The city which grew most rapidly and insalubriously was Glasgow. At the end of the first quarter of the eighteenth century it had only 13,000 inhabitants. Its polarities were the Cathedral and the University; it was a city of orchards and gardens, with one medieval bridge spanning its clean river. By 1740 there were 17,000 people in Glasgow, and in 1745 its growing prosperity led it to receive Prince Charles Edward Stuart, on his retreat from Derby, with terrified reluctance. Glasgow wanted neither to be forced to contribute to the Jacobite coffers nor to be indemnified for favouring the Rising. Until the end of the eighteenth century the population and the prosperity of Glasgow continued more or less in step; but the development of heavy industries in the Clydeside area attracted more and more impoverished Highlanders and Irishmen in search of employment. There were 77,000 people in Glasgow by 1800; by 1830 there were over 200,000. The Irish Potato Famine brought another immense influx of desperate immigrants, so that by 1860 the population was over 390,000. It continued to grow, and had reached 1,000,000 by 1911.

While increasing numbers crowded into tenements

and cellars, without water or sanitation, epidemic diseases brought an appallingly high mortality rate, without checking the growth of population. Smallpox was the worst killer disease during the greater part of the eighteenth century, especially in the slums of the cities. But it was also a scourge of country districts, including remote areas of the Highlands. In some places experiments in inoculation were carried out, and some local inoculators enjoyed considerable reputations. But prevention of smallpox did not become generally effective until the introduction of vaccination by Edward Jenner. 10,000 people were vaccinated in Glasgow between 1801 and 1806, and the drop in the smallpox mortality rate was so impressive that people began to imagine that the disease had been conquered. They ceased to trouble to be vaccinated, with the result that there were renewed outbreaks of smallpox in 1817 and 1818. By the mid-nineteenth century crowded cities faced a new threat in the spread of cholera to Europe from the Far East. The first appearance of cholera in Glasgow was in the autumn of 1831, and renewed outbreaks occurred in 1848 and 1849, and again in 1853 and 1866. The results of this epidemic led at last to the introduction of a Public Health Act, framed with special reference to Scotland, in 1867. It was none too soon, for Edwin Chadwick, whose great work in improving sanitation did so much for public health in England, said that he had never seen misery to equal that of Glasgow in any other British city.

In the earlier eighteenth century, when Glasgow was described as 'odoriferous' with orchards and gardens, Edinburgh had a less salubrious reputation. The medieval city, which had grown along the ridge descending from the Castle to the Abbey of Holyrood, had not expanded greatly during the ensuing centuries. To the north of the Castle and the city lay the Nor' Loch, which had always created a natural barrier to expansion. Extension to the south had been an unattractive proposition during the centuries of strife with England: no one would have wanted to live in a vulnerable suburb which would have been the first target for the invaders to burn. In consequence, Edinburgh grew upwards. The tall stone tenements, or 'lands' of the Old Town, were ten or twelve storeys high, and they housed all classes of the population. On the first and second floors were the lodgings of noblemen, lairds, professors and judges; above them lived a cross-section of the populace, of whom the only generalization to be made was that 'the lowest shall be highest'. On the common stair of any land the inhabitants passed one another in close enough proximity to become well acquainted. Acquaintance-ship may not have led to egalitarianism, but at least class distinctions were blurred by neighbourliness. They were also blurred by general uncleanliness. 'Sir,' said Dr Johnson, when he visited James Boswell in Edinburgh in 1773, 'I smell you in the dark', and anyone could have said the same to anyone else.

In the years following 1745 the cramped and insanitary city became the scene of an increasingly lively intellectual life. Some credit for its early begin-nings belongs to Allan Ramsay the elder, son of the superintendent of the lead and gold mines at Leadhill in Lanarkshire, who was apprenticed to a wig maker in Edinburgh in 1700. Ramsay became a poet and a bookseller, and in 1725 he opened the first circulating library in Scotland. He tried to found a theatre, but ecclesiastical disapproval prevented him. However, his enthusiasm for the stage led him to provide his customers with dramatic texts, including the works of Dryden, and to write a Scots pastoral comedy entitled *The Gentle Shepherd*, which has been successfully revived. Allan Ramsay the younger was sent by his prosperous father on the Grand Tour, in the course of which he studied painting in Italy. On his return to Britain he gained a great reputation as a portrait painter, both in London and Edinburgh. The younger Ramsay, however, also inherited his father's love of literature, and in 1754 he founded the Select Society for Encouraging Art, Science and Industry, which appealed to some of the most brilliant men of the age, among them David Hume, Adam Smith, and the brothers Adam, the family of architects, of whom Robert, the most gifted, was to design many buildings in the New Town of Edinburgh.

The long-needed expansion of Edinburgh began slowly, and at first did not arouse any great enthusiasm, because no one wished to exile himself from the centre of society to the other side of the Nor' Loch, which had long ceased to be a beautiful sheet of water and become a fetid marsh, filled with the city's refuse. The drainage of the Nor' Loch was undertaken in 1770, followed by the longer task of filling the bed of it. In the meantime the North Bridge was built across the bed of the Loch, and the two halves of the city were given easy access to each other. The first New Town, completed in the early years of the nineteenth century to the design of James Craig, consisted of the broad, straight thoroughfare of George Street, linking St Andrew Square at its eastern end and Charlotte Square at its western end. South of George Street, Princes Street was built facing the craggy profile of the Old

Town, and north of George Street, the parallel Queen Street. The second New Town, begun in the 1820s, extended northward from Queen Street, sloping downhill from Queen Street Gardens, in parallels from Heriot Row to Fettes Row, its symmetry completed at the west by Moray Place, and at the east by Drummond Place. Long before all of it was built, as R. L. Stevenson wrote:

> ... when the New Town began to spread abroad its draughty parallelograms and rear its long frontage on the opposing hill, there was such a flitting, such a change of domicile and dweller as was never excelled in the history of cities.

In the Old Town, 'the cobbler succeeded the earl; the beggar ensconced himself by the judge's chimney; what had been a palace was used as a pauper refuge'. It remained for twentieth-century urban conservationists to rescue the slum dwellings of the Old Town and restore some of the old lands to their former dignity, and to provide them with comforts which they had never possessed in their heyday.

Among the first to join the great 'flitting' of aristocracy, intellect and fashion to the New Town was David Hume, the greatest luminary of the Scottish Enlightenment, of whom it was said that the street in which he made his new home was named 'David Street' in his honour, and nicknamed 'St David Street', a tribute to his personal popularity, and a gentle gibe at his philosophical scepticism. Whatever the truth of the story, the street is 'St David Street'.

The group of brilliant men whose writings, whose mutually inspiring society, and whose stimulating effect on their contemporaries constituted the Scottish Enlightenment, was not in any self-conscious sense a group or a movement. An historian of France has written:

> Although the Enlightenment in France consisted of a series of individuals who were very different one from another, they together constituted a formidable challenge to the existing social and political order.

The same could be said of the Enlightenment in Scotland. Those who contributed to it subjected everything which was accepted through habit or hallowed by tradition – religion, law, government, the social order, the laws of nature – to question, and to reasoned examination.

Hume's *Treatise on Human Nature* (1739), *Essays Moral and Political* (1741), *Philosophical Essays Concerning Human Understanding* (1748) and *Enquiry Concerning the Principles of Morals* (1751), won him great esteem in France, where he was Secretary to the British Embassy in Paris, and for a time Chargé d'Affaires. His subjection of Christian philosophy to logic influenced a new generation of philosophers and disturbed the theologically unquestioning among his own compatriots. Hume's younger friend, Adam Smith, was the author of *An Inquiry into the Nature and Causes of the Wealth of Nations* (1776), the parent text of the modern study of economic theory, the publication of which has been described as 'the most remarkable intellectual event of the 1770s'. Smith advocated free trade, and his book profoundly influenced the younger Pitt, who became Prime Minister in 1784. Indeed, his influence remained paramount, and in the words of a modern Scottish historian, he continued to be 'the patron saint of British economic policy until, in the twentieth century, free trade was abandoned and governmental policy reverted to controls and restrictions similar to those which Smith had condemned'.

Scottish intellectual activity was extraordinarily diverse. James Hutton in 1785 published his *Theory of the Earth*, a foundation work in geology, and he also investigated meteorology in *The Theory of Rain*. Sir John Sinclair of Ulbster initiated the production of the first *Statistical Account of Scotland*, which was published in twenty-one volumes in 1799, a work which was pioneering in statistics and is invaluable to historians. William Robertson, historian, and later Principal of Edinburgh University, impressed Horace Walpole so much with his *History of Scotland during the Reigns of Mary and James VI* (1759), that Walpole wrote:

How could I suspect that a man under forty whose dialect I scarce understood . . . had not only written what all the world now allows to be the best modern history, but that he had written it in the purest English and with as much seeming knowledge of men and courts as if he had passed all his life in important embassies?

The cosmopolitan Hume seems to have been equally surprised at the respect which Scottish scholarship aroused: 'Is it not strange,' he wrote, 'that, at a time when we have lost our Princes, our Parliaments, our independent Government, even the presence of our chief nobility, are unhappy in our accent and pronunciation, speak a very corrupt dialect of the tongue which we make use of; is it not strange, I say, that, in these circumstances, we should really be the people most distinguished for literature in Europe?'

Hume did not overestimate the respect with which the works of the Scottish Enlightenment were internationally regarded. The Scottish philosophers, like the *philosophes* of France, were at the forefront of the intellectual movements of their time, forming, stimulating and provoking the opinions of their politically conscious countrymen and of their students. They did not all speak with the same voice. Adam Fergusson, who became Professor of Moral Philosophy in the University of Edinburgh in 1764, was one of the Commissioners sent to America to attempt to persuade the colonists to reconsider the Declaration of Independence. Dugald Stewart, who succeeded Fergusson as Professor of Moral Philosophy in 1785, was considered to hold such radical views that when the French Revolution came, the parents of some of his students forbade their sons to attend his lectures.

In Scotland the American War of Independence and the French Revolution in turn aroused the greatest intellectual excitement. Many Scots followed the events of the American War of Independence with ardent sympathy, an indication that they were beginning to equate the predicament of the American colonists with their own. The excitement aroused by the early stages of the French Revolution suggested a strong general response to the attractive doctrines of the *Déclaration des Droits de l'Homme*. But though the Scottish Enlightenment inspired intellectual questioning and aroused pro-revolutionary fervour, it did not lead to the transformation of Scottish society. On the contrary, the radical ferment which the Enlightenment at home and the revolutionary wars abroad inspired resulted in violent repressive measures in Scotland. Even non-violent movements in favour of parliamentary reform, which was increasingly necessary in Scotland as the century progressed, were regarded as being revolutionary in spirit. Advocates of reform were suspected of holding dangerously radical views, and the more outspoken of them were persecuted as revolutionaries.

The most celebrated of the so-called 'Political Martyrs' was Thomas Muir of Huntershill, who was a founder member of a society for parliamentary reform in Glasgow in 1792. In 1793 he was tried for 'exciting a spirit of disloyalty and disaffection' and for recommending Tom Paine's *The Rights of Man*. Muir, together with his fellow 'Political Martyrs', Magarot, Gerrald and Skirving, was tried before one of the most famous of Scottish judges, the notoriously severe Lord Braxfield, and sentenced to fourteen years' transportation to the Australian penal colony of Botany Bay. As a political trial, the trial of Thomas Muir retains its importance; it maintains its drama because it was a clash of personalities. Muir eventually escaped from Australia, and after an extraordinary series of adventures in Mexico and Cuba, reached France, where he died, hailed as a hero by the *Directoire*. Braxfield, immortalized in fiction by R.L. Stevenson as Weir of Hermiston, was a paradoxical character: aggressively Scots in speech and manners, in his own opinion a patriot, yet an implacable enemy of the radicalism in which Scots patriotism also sought to express itself.

With the rise of Napoleon, Scottish enthusiasm for

the French Revolution, which might not have been killed off by the severe punishment of men suspected of revolutionary sentiments, died a natural death. The Napoleonic Wars produced a new British patriotism, which for the first time inspired both Scots and English to identify their interests against a potential invader. This Anglo-Scottish political alignment might not have happened so readily if Scottish political life had not stagnated since the Union. While this stagnation seems strangely incongruous with the liveliness of Scottish intellectual life, it is not really so very surprising, because the opportunities for men with political ambitions were extremely few.

As previously mentioned, a very small number of the Scottish peers had the right to sit in the House of Lords, and the forty-five Scottish members of the House of Commons were elected on the basis of a very narrow franchise. Of these forty-five members, thirty represented the counties, and fifteen represented the sixty-five Royal Burghs. In the counties the franchise was still based on the medieval concept of Parliament as an assembly of the tenants-in-chief of the Crown, and by the late eighteenth century there were very few of them. In 1788 there were less than 3000 men in Scotland with the right to vote. The members who sat for the Royal Burghs were elected on a particularly circumscribed franchise: by delegates who were chosen for the purpose of voting by groups of four or five burghs. The very small total of voters made the political management of Scotland in the interest of the Government of the day perfectly feasible. The Government had almost unlimited means of winning the support of voters, especially as the secret ballot had not yet been introduced. A voter who engaged to support

a Whig or Tory candidate – for example, in return for
army promotion or ecclesiastical patronage for a son
– could not renege on election day. The political
management of Scotland, obnoxious as it now seems,
was smoothly organized, and probably created a great
deal of satisfaction in the form of the sum of individual
gratitude.

The most powerful of a series of 'managers' was
Henry Dundas, first Viscount Melville, who became
Lord Advocate in 1775. Dundas's effective rule of
Scotland in the Tory interest lasted until 1805, during
which time he was successively Treasurer of the Navy,
Home Secretary, President of the Board of Control for
India, Secretary for War, and First Lord of the
Admiralty. This range of ministerial appointments
mirrors Dundas's very real ability, and his capacity for
taking on an almost incredible burden of work.
Naturally, in the context of his times, Dundas used the
opportunities for political patronage which his posts
provided to increase his influence in Scotland. He was
able to control the results of elections in at least
thirty-six of the forty-five Scottish constituencies. In
1796 he achieved a total of thirty-nine.

Dundas's English political opponents criticized his
consistent advancement of his own countrymen,
especially in India; but advancement was not given to
ambitious Scots without assurance of their ability.
Dundas's reign as 'Uncrowned King of Scotland'
ended in 1805, when he resigned on being accused of
malversation of Admiralty funds. An attempt to
impeach him failed, and he was able to retire with
honour in 1806. His popularity in Scotland was
illustrated by the fact that in his own country even his
political opponents rejoiced at his acquittal. It is not

easy to see Dundas as other than a corrupt politician, for what is now regarded as a very crude form of corruption was the means by which he retained power; yet it was for an entirely different form of corruption that he was unsuccessfully attacked, and his power was consistently exercised in the interests of Scotland, as he saw them. However, Dundas could only be an opponent of parliamentary reform, which would have struck at the root of his system of management.

When the much-needed Reform Bill of 1832 was passed, it increased the number of Scottish Members of Parliament and the scope of the franchise. Eight new constituencies were created, bringing the total of Scottish MPs to fifty-three. Edinburgh and Glasgow were represented by two members each, and Paisley, Greenock, Dundee, Aberdeen and Perth by one each. In the burghs the franchise was extended to all householders who paid £10 in rates, and in the counties it was extended to owners of property valued at £10 and to leaseholders of property valued at £50, and leased for not less than nineteen years. This was a cautious beginning, but the Electoral Reform Bill of 1868 extended the franchise again to include all burgh householders, and increased the number of Scottish MPs to sixty. Thenceforward, voters were no longer men of substance only; many of them were wage-earners whose political opinions could put them at the mercy of their employers. The Secret Ballot Act of 1872 was an essential extension of their enfranchisement. Adult male suffrage was introduced in 1884, and at the same time the number of MPs was again increased, to seventy-two. Votes for women over the age of thirty followed in 1918, and for those over the age of twenty-one in 1928.

So long as the vast majority of the Scottish people remained unenfranchised it was not surprising that in general they took little interest in politics. However, what the Scots lacked in political awareness, they made up for by a passionate concern with religious affairs. In a sense their concern was religio-political, deriving its inspiration from Andrew Melville's doctrine of the Two Kingdoms, Spiritual and Temporal, of which the former was superior, and must be independent. That the claim of the Spiritual Kingdom had not been satisfied by the Presbyterian Establishment of 1690, and had been flouted by the Patronage Act of 1712, was the basic cause of the troubles which beset the religious life of Scotland during the eighteenth and nineteenth centuries.

The Government ignored a series of protests by the General Assembly against the Patronage Act, and in consequence a number of ministers, followed by their congregations, left the established Church in the 'Original Secession' of 1733. But the seceders were soon faced with a new moral dilemma as to whether burgesses should take an oath to uphold 'the true Protestant religion presently professed within this realm' – was not that an oath to uphold the state Church which they had abjured? They divided into 'Burghers' and 'Anti-Burghers', in 1747. The Burghers then fell out over the question of whether the Solemn League and Covenant was still a living issue, or had become irrelevant: the 'Auld Lichts' thought the former, and the 'New Lichts' the latter. A disagreement over the consecration of the bread and wine for the Lord's Supper followed: 'Lifters' thought that they should be elevated for the consecration, 'Anti-Lifters' thought that they should not. When the Original

Secession Church had almost dissolved itself with scruples, the Second Secession occurred in 1761, and the 'Relief Church' was formed, with the resolves that it would neither submit to patronage nor receive state support, but that each congregation should support its kirk and its minister.

With the Second Secession, the fissionary tendency of the established Church seemed to have been exhausted. During the later eighteenth century a dominant party in the General Assembly accommodated itself to the position of a state Church, and accepted patronage and the necessity of supportive oaths. These non-fanatical ministers were aptly named 'Moderates'. Their relaxed, though perfectly moral standards of ministerial conduct would have outraged the ministers of the Covenanting period. The Moderates dined in Edinburgh society, played cards, and attended the theatre, which had existed in Edinburgh despite ministerial disapproval since 1747. Relations between the Church and the theatre underwent a startling change when David Hume's cousin, the Reverend John Home (who to the philosopher's disgust adopted the aristocratic spelling of their surname), wrote an immensely successful tragedy *Douglas*, which was performed at the Canongate Theatre in 1756. At the time, Home was censured by the General Assembly, and William Robertson, then at the beginning of his career, was one of only eleven ministers who defended Home. But times changed, and when the great tragedian Sarah Siddons visited Edinburgh in 1784, the sessions of the General Assembly were scheduled so as not to clash with the times of her performances, which many ministers wished to attend. One of her most successful parts was that of Lady Randolph in Home's *Douglas*!

The Moderates were also typical of their times in other ways: they exalted reason, read the works of Hume, and found religious enthusiasm and theological fanaticism equally tasteless. They provoked an opposition in the 'Evangelicals', who possessed all the enthusiasm which the Moderates disliked, and who were rightly concerned at the godless condition of the rapidly growing populations of the industrial cities. The Evangelicals had the advantage which reformers always have over defenders of the status quo: that they could challenge entrenched and comfortable passivity with the promise of improvement.

The Evangelicals challenged the Moderates on the patronage issue. In 1834 the Evangelicals introduced the Veto Act into the General Assembly, which proposed that if a majority of the heads of families in a parish rejected the minister nominated by the patron, their rejection should be sufficient grounds for his non-admission. The Veto Act was passed by a majority of the General Assembly, and it precipitated a crisis. The law courts did not uphold the Veto Act, and so the question of the Two Kingdoms, Spiritual and Temporal, was raised again, in a new guise. In May 1843 a majority of Evangelicals, dissatisfied with compromise measures which had been offered during the preceding nine years, left the General Assembly, and under the leadership of Dr Thomas Chalmers, founded the Free Church of Scotland. The 474 ministers who took part in the 'Disruption', the last and greatest of the Secessions, formed over a third of the total number of ministers, and since they were followed by their congregations, they immediately provided the Free

Church with a formidable membership. The ministers of the Free Church abandoned their kirks, their manses and their stipends, on grounds of principle; but a parish organization which duplicated that of the established Church was quickly developed. Free Church kirks, manses and schools were built, some of them endowed by industrialists whose employees were supporters of the Free Church.

Sectarian rivalry led to rivalry in good works, especially in the field of foreign missions. However, there was opportunity for missionary activity without seeking it overseas. Parts of the Highlands, especially the remote areas of the north-west, had not been reached by the Reformation, and the decay of Catholicism had left them without any continuous spiritual care. Irish Franciscans had conducted missions in the first half of the seventeenth century, but though they claimed many converts they had been unable to sustain their efforts. The Protestant missionaries of the later eighteenth century attempted to be more systematic. In 1767 the Scottish Society for Propagating Christian Knowledge published the first New Testament in Gaelic, an achievement contrary to Government policy, since at this period every expression of Gaelic life was discouraged because of its connection with Jacobitism.

Throughout most of the eighteenth century the Episcopal Church of Scotland suffered from its Jacobite connections. When Jacobitism itself ceased to be a living political cause, after the death of Prince Charles Edward Stuart, toleration was at last extended to 'non-juring' Episcopalians – those who had refused to swear loyalty to the Hanoverian monarch. By the time that the Penal Laws against the non-juring Episcopalians were repealed in 1792, their Church had become no more than 'a shadow of a shade', in the words of Sir Walter Scott. However, while the Episcopal Church of Scotland was at its weakest, it played an influential role in the spiritual life of the Episcopal Church in America. During the American War of Independence, Samuel Seabury, elected bishop by the Episcopalian clergy of Connecticut, was refused consecration in England, and, in order to ensure the Apostolic Succession for his Church, he visited Aberdeen, and received the rite at the hands of three 'pious and venerable bishops of Scotland', in 1783.

Religious life of considerable diversity provided the Scots with a means of national self-expression while access to political life was largely denied them, but nonetheless, the identity of Scotland might yet have become merged with that of England, had it not been for a new literature which both expressed the Scottish national consciousness and gained an international appeal. While David Hume had marvelled that a people unhappy in their accent and pronunciation and speaking a very corrupt dialect of the tongue that they made use of could become the people most distinguished for literature in Europe, a different trend was developing. Scottish prose is often said to have suffered from the fact that at the Reformation the Scots received the Bible in an English translation, so that a Scots equivalent of the Authorized Version never had a ~~correspondingly healthy influence on the Scots vernacular.~~

Certainly, throughout the sixteenth and seventeenth centuries there was a progressive anglicization of prose in Lowland Scotland, which left the vernacular to survive as a spoken language. Nonetheless, in that form it retained its vigour, and revived as a language of poetry.

Allan Ramsay the elder and Robert Fergusson were the precursors of Robert Burns in the revival of Scots as a literary language; but Burns was the genius who re-established it. As Shakespeare is the national poet of the English, Burns is the national poet of the Scots; but Burns has a wider social appeal, for his work demands a less intellectual response. Though it has been said of him by a distinguished modern Scots poet that he 'gets through to don and docker equally', the harshest criticism levelled against him is that he deals 'only in the great platitudes'. Paradoxically, this may be the essence of his genius and his appeal. Though his words are appreciated by the profound, he also expresses the thoughts which inarticulate men think, or suddenly recognize that they ought to think, and then they delight to quote him:

> Then gently scan your brother Man,
>   Still gentler sister Woman;
> Tho' they may gang a kennin* wrang,
>   To step aside is human . . .

Burns responded with magnificently quotable simplicity to the aspirations of the revolutionary period, when he wrote in 1794:

> . . . let us pray that come it may,
>   As come it will for a' that,
> That sense and worth, o'er a' the earth,
>   May bear the gree,† and a' that.
> For a' that, and a' that,

*knowing
†win the victory

> It's comin yet for a' that,
> That man to man, the warld o'er,
> Shall brothers be for a' that.

Yet, at the same time, Burns could respond to the nostalgic appeal of Jacobitism, and look back to a remoter past, as when he inscribed on the window-pane of an inn at Stirling:

> Here Stuarts once in glory reigned,
> And laws for Scotland's weal ordained;
> But now unroof'd their palace stands,
> Their sceptre fallen to other hands...

Not surprisingly, Burns has been accused of muddled political thinking, of being simultaneously 'Jacobin and Jacobite'; but yet another aspect of his appeal may be that on the profoundly emotive subjects of radicalism and historical nostalgia, he can be equally eloquent. Burns spoke for humanity, and for Scotland. He satirized folly and hypocrisy, and he celebrated love and friendship in such universal terms that his works gained an audience far beyond the borders of Scotland, or of Britain itself. In the present century they have been translated into Russian, Japanese and Chinese; even in his own century, his immense success contributed to a renewed awareness that though Scotland and England might be united, their national characters were not.

Burns's stature as one of the world's poets has been gradually growing. The international success of Sir Walter Scott was immediate. Scott's first success was as a narrative poet, with *The Lay of the Last Minstrel*, published in 1805, followed by *Marmion, The Lady of the Lake*, and *The Lord of the Isles*. In 1814 he published *Waverley*, the first of his great series of historical novels. Reaction to it in Edinburgh was described by the memoirist Lord Cockburn:

> The unexpected newness of the thing, the profusion of the original characters, the Scotch language, Scotch scenery, Scotch men and women, the simplicity of the writing and the graphic force of the descriptions – all struck us with a shock of delight.

Other novels followed in rapid succession, among them *The Antiquary* and *Old Mortality*, in 1816; *Rob Roy* and *The Heart of Midlothian* in 1818; and in 1819 *The Bride of Lammermoor*, on which Donizetti based his immensely successful opera *Lucia di Lammermoor*, composed in 1836. The 'shock of delight' which had greeted *Waverley* continued to greet Scott's novels, which, in the words of a recent historian, 'gave Scotland back her history, a history of which all could be proud and in which all could see themselves and their forebears in a dramatic and romantic, if occasionally somewhat idealized light'. This would have been a rare achievement for any novelist, but Scott did more: he reintroduced the Scots and their history to the English, in the same somewhat idealized light. In so doing, he broke down an historic prejudice, and in his vast English readership he replaced ancient hostility to the Scots with romantic admiration for them.

At the height of his fame, in 1822, Scott organized the state visit of King George IV to Scotland. There has been tasteless repetition in ridiculing the King's attempt to appeal to the Scots by wearing Highland dress. His portrait, in a kilt of Royal Stewart tartan, painted by Sir David Wilkie, shows him looking theatrical and ill-at-ease, and perpetuates the tradition that the royal visit was an occasion of absurdity; but perhaps, if George IV had been painted by Sir Henry Raeburn, whom he knighted during his stay in Edinburgh, posterity might have thought of it differently. Raeburn's superb portraits of the famous Scots of his generation – including David Hume, Adam Smith, Dugald Stewart, Sinclair of Ulbster, Lord Braxfield, Henry Dundas, and Sir Walter Scott himself – never lacked either dignity or insight. Historical insight, in an attempt to make good the lack, might suggest that since George IV's visit to Scotland was only the second to have been made by a member of the Hanoverian dynasty – the first having been that of the Duke of Cumberland – it was a gesture of reconciliation which deserved to have been accepted with the generosity of spirit in which it was conceived.

Though George IV's decision to wear Highland dress on his visit to Scotland may have been a flamboyant gesture on his part, it was a decision which belonged to the mood of the period. The Dress Act had been repealed under the Dundas regime, in 1783, and thereafter the very fact that it had been forbidden led to its adoption as a national dress. As a symbol of Scottishness, it was worn by Lowlanders, who formerly would have despised it. George IV, by wearing it, was attempting to present himself to his Scottish subjects dressed not as King of Great Britain, but as King of Scots. Though his personal popularity was not much enhanced, his example did not fail to increase the popularity of Highland dress, which in one form or another has remained part of the world of fashion ever since.

During the years of proscription Highland dress had continued to exist as the uniform of the Highland Regiments in the service of the Government. The first of these had been the Independent Companies raised by General Wade during his period as Commander-in-Chief in the Highlands. Recruited from the clans which supported the Government, the Companies were formed into the 42nd Regiment – the Black Watch. During the Seven Years' War (1756–63), when Britain's military resources were strained to the limit, the elder Pitt decided to enlist Highlanders irrespective of their former political affiliations. Since the Middle Ages Highlanders had been accustomed to fight as soldiers of fortune, and they proved ready to offer their traditional loyalty and professionalism to the British Government. In 1766, Pitt justified his experiment in a well-known speech to the House of Commons:

> I sought for merit wherever it was to be found. It is my boast that I was the first Minister who looked for it and found it in the mountains of the north. I called it forth and drew into your service a hardy and intrepid race of men . . . They served with fidelity as they fought with valour and conquered for you in every part of the world.

The achievements of the Highland Regiments contributed to the metamorphosis of the Highlander in popular estimation from the feared and detested 'Wild Scot' into a pattern of heroism.

That the Highlander also became a figure of romance

resulted from the influence of the 'Celtic Revival', an aspect of the Romantic Movement which owed much to the works of Scott, but probably more to those of James Macpherson. In 1760 Macpherson published *Fragments of Ancient Poetry, Collected in the Highlands and Translated from the Gaelic* which was enthusiastically received by David Hume and William Robertson, amongst others. Macpherson followed it in 1762 with *Fingal, an Ancient Epic Poem ... Composed by Ossian*, which he also claimed to have translated from the Gaelic. It enjoyed an immense success (which included that of becoming one of Napoleon's favourite books), but Dr Johnson shrewdly expressed his doubts of it, and Macpherson's reputation subsequently suffered from the fact that he failed to produce his Gaelic originals. Nonetheless, he stimulated an increasing interest in Highland life, and in the Gaelic traditions of the past. Yet, as an aspect of a general revival of Scottish national consciousness, the Celtic Revival was extraordinary because it expressed enthusiasm for a style of life which was decaying even while it was being romanticized *in memoriam*, and for a style of life which Lowlanders could only regard with nostalgia when it had ceased to be threatening to the established order which Lowland life had for so long represented.

While the Celtic Revival made the Highlands fashionable, improved communications made them unprecedentedly accessible. In 1802 the great engineer Thomas Telford was commissioned to report on the roads, bridges and fisheries of the Highlands. As a result of his report, Telford was given charge of a programme of improvements which resulted in the construction of 920 miles of roads, 1200 bridges, improvements of many existing harbours, and, most remarkable of all, the creation of the Caledonian Canal. Railway building also contributed to the opening up of the Highlands, though not to the approval of everyone. In 1845, Lord Cockburn wrote: 'Britain is at present an isle of lunatics all railway-mad. The patients are raving even in the wild recesses of the Highlands.'

The new accessibility, and the interest stimulated by the Celtic Revival, drew Queen Victoria and Prince Albert to visit the Highlands for the first time in 1842. In 1848 they took a lease of Balmoral Castle, and bought it four years later. Their ardently enthusiastic response to the beauty of the Highlands, and their establishment of a royal residence there, at first enhanced the fashion for the Celtic Revival, but in the end contributed to its decline. The castle was elaborately rebuilt in the 'Scottish Baronial' style, and the interior was furnished with Royal Stewart and Hunting Stewart tartan carpets, Dress Stewart curtains and thistle-patterned chintzes. At the time of its creation, a lady of more discerning taste than the Queen described it as 'all highly characteristic, but not all equally *flatteuse* to the eye'. The Balmoral style was imitated in castles and houses all over Scotland, until a revulsion against 'Balmorality' occurred after Queen Victoria's death.

This revulsion was an obvious rejection of an essentially romantic expression of the Scottish national consciousness, which had served a useful purpose in displaying the identity of Scotland when it was endangered, but which had proved an inadequate means of continuing either to express it or to defend it.

It is difficult to assign a date to a national change of heart, because such an occurrence is neither immediate nor unanimous. But, whereas from approximately the mid-eighteenth to the mid-nineteenth century the great majority of Scots had been content that politically Scotland should be no more than North Britain, from the mid-nineteenth century onwards, a cultural identity began to seem an increasingly unsatisfactory expression of Scottish nationhood to an ever-growing number of Scots.

CHAPTER NINE

Scotland in the Modern World
1850 – 1982

After the Union, but especially from the mid-eighteenth century onwards, Scots participated in the achievements of Great Britain so outstandingly that it might have seemed that the aspirations of the Scottish nation were being abundantly fulfilled by its representatives. For centuries Scots had gone abroad and distinguished themselves in the service of foreign powers, but Scottish participation in the expansion of the British Empire, in exploration, missionary work and imperial administration gave more and more Scots opportunities to pursue their ambitions in remoter parts of the world than their compatriots had reached in earlier centuries.

A handful of examples will serve to illustrate Scottish achievements in all continents of the world. Scottish exploration of Africa was pioneered by Mungo Park, who was born in Selkirkshire in 1771. He undertook a voyage of exploration in search of the source of the River Niger in 1795, and wrote his classic *Travels in the Interior of Africa* in 1799. His fate was never known with complete certainty, but he is believed to have been murdered by hostile tribesmen during his second voyage up the Niger in 1806. Remote parts of Canada were opened to Scottish enterprise by Sir Alexander Mackenzie, who was born at Inverness in about 1755, and spent his early life at

Stromness in Orkney. As a young man he joined the North West Fur Company, founded as a rival to the Hudson's Bay Company (most of whose employees were Orcadians). In the service of the North West Fur Company, Mackenzie made two great voyages of exploration, the first in 1789 to the Arctic Ocean, and the second in 1793 across the Rocky Mountains to the Pacific coast. His *Voyages on the River St Lawrence and Through the Continent of North America to the Frozen and Pacific Oceans* was dedicated to George III. Mackenzie was knighted in 1802, and died in retirement in Scotland in 1820. Australia was the scene of the remarkable later career of Lachlan Macquarie, eldest son of the chief of the Clan Macquarrie, born on the Isle of Ulva at an uncertain date. He joined the 84th Regiment of Foot in 1777, and his military service took him to Nova Scotia, America, Jamaica, India, Cochin China (now part of Vietnam), Egypt and Ceylon, before he became Governor of the Convict Settlement of New South Wales in Australia. His authoritarian government and extravagant spending on public works made him many enemies, but his effort to integrate into society convicts whose sentences had been completed was extremely enlightened. He directed explor ation although he did not participate in it, and Macquarie Island, south of Tasmania, discovered in ... ... one of the many places named in his honour. Probably even in the ... ... century, few people have served their country in so many parts of the world.

The greatest of Scottish explorers, and surely one of the greatest servants of humanity, was the missionary doctor David Livingstone, born at Blantyre, Lanark- shire, in 1813. Livingstone's almost incredibly arduous journeys in Africa, inspired by the desire to spread Christianity and to combat the slave trade, led him to the discovery of Lake Nyasa and the Victoria Falls. He told his own story in *Missionary Travels and Researches in South Africa* (1857), *Narrative of an Expedition to the Zambesi and its Tributaries* (1865), and his *Last Journals* were published in 1874, the year after his death.

In India, as previously mentioned, many Scots gained advancement in the East India Company through the good offices of Henry Dundas. After the Indian Mutiny of 1857, when India came under the direct rule of the British Parliament, Scots staffed all ranks of the Indian Civil Service, and Scottish Viceroys of India were the eighth and ninth Earls of Elgin, the fourth Earl of Minto and the eleventh Earl of Dalhousie. The characteristic intellectualism of Scottish men of action was remarkably exemplified by the brothers Cunningham, who made their careers in the Indian Army and distinguished themselves as scholars. Sir Alexander Cunningham reached the rank of Major-General, and after his retirement was director general of the Indian Archaeological Survey from 1870 to 1885. During his last years he wrote studies of Indian numismatics, his great enthusiasm. His brother Joseph Cunningham was less fortunate. While still a serving officer he wrote a much acclaimed *History of the Sikhs* (1849), but the accusation that he had incorporated in it secret information acquired in the course of his military and political duties led to his disgrace, and consequent early death.

Possibly the most famous of all Scots who made their careers abroad was an individualist who defies all categorization, the millionaire and philanthropist

Andrew Carnegie. He was born in Dunfermline in 1835, the son of a linen weaver who was forced by poverty to emigrate to Pennsylvania in 1848. Andrew Carnegie, from such humble beginnings as a telegraph messenger boy and a clerk, eventually amassed a vast fortune on the Pennsylvania Railroad and in steel manufacture, and made the astonishing pronouncement that 'the man who dies rich dies disgraced.' Between 1901 and his death in 1919 he distributed his fortune of £60,000,000 in a great variety of benefactions, one of which was the Carnegie Trust for the Universities of Scotland, which provided amongst other purposes, scholarships for students of Scottish birth or extraction. Carnegie had a typically Scottish inclination to tell his own story and wrote a number of books, including *The Gospel of Wealth* (1900), in which he elaborated the doctrine expressed in his famous dictum, and his *Autobiography*, which was published the year following his death.

The achievements of Scots abroad belong to the history of Scotland for a particularly significant reason: they are remembered as 'Scottish' and not as 'British' achievements. Despite the Union, with all its integrating pressures, Scots retained their sense of nationality, even in the most distant continents of the world. The same is true of the many thousands of nameless Scots who were progenitors of populations of Scottish descent in Canada, America, Australia and New Zealand, which by now far outnumber the population of the parent country. All these descendants of Scottish emigrants retain either a sense of nationality or else a strong attachment to Scotland, which they display by visiting it in great numbers in search of their ancestral roots, or to see the places of their origin.

It was not the Scots who went abroad, but those who remained at home who felt that the survival of their nationhood was threatened. By the mid-nineteenth century the Union had been almost universally accepted in Scotland for a hundred years. But thereafter its desirability was increasingly called in question. Though the first one hundred and fifty years of the Union had been in many ways years of great achievement, many unsolved problems remained – urban poverty, the appalling conditions of industrial workers, the ruined economy of the Highlands, the splintering of the Presbyterian Church – for which the Union was increasingly held responsible. Critics of the Union blamed the British Parliament for neglect or misgovernment of Scotland. In 1851 the Convention of Royal Burghs drew up a memorandum on the neglect of Scottish affairs, and in 1853 the National Association for the Vindication of Scottish Rights was founded. The latter has been somewhat contemptuously dismissed by a modern Scottish historian as a 'Movement . . . inspired partly at least by middle class romanticism', but, if this were true it would not be surprising, as the romanticism of the Celtic Revival had done much to reawaken the national spirit, and the Reform Bill of 1832 had enfranchised the middle class. The romantic element was represented by Professor W.E. Aytoun, author of a well-loved collection of historical poems, *Lays of the Scottish Cavaliers*. But the Association was also supported by the Lords Provost both of Edinburgh and Glasgow, and public meetings in the two cities attracted attendances of 2000 and 5000 people respectively. The National Association for the Vindication of Scottish Rights demanded a Secretary of State for Scotland and more Scottish MPs, and deplored the small amount of public money spent on Scotland. Though its demands were modest and its existence short – it was dissolved in 1856, possibly as a result of the deflection of public interest by the Crimean War – it expressed a dissatisfaction with the way in which Scotland was governed which grew with the passage of time.

Though the National Association for the Vindication of Scottish Rights was short-lived, its aims were not forgotten. A period of more overtly nationalistic activity began in the 1880s. The demand for a Scottish Secretary was satisfied in 1885, though he was not at first accorded ministerial rank. But in the meantime Home Rule both for Scotland and Ireland had become important parliamentary issues, and the appointment of a Scottish Secretary, which would have given some satisfaction when it was first demanded, seemed only a minor concession when it was granted. Renewed dissatisfaction showed itself with the foundation of the Scottish Home Rule Association in 1886. By this time the electoral reforms of 1868 and 1884 had widened the franchise, and together with the introduction of the secret ballot, had completely changed the political complexion of Scotland.

The end of political management brought the end of the Tory ascendancy which it had ensured. Electoral reform was followed by a long Liberal ascendancy. The Scottish Liberals were supporters of Home Rule, since its introduction could be expected to keep them in office for a long time to come. In England, Liberal support for the cause of Home Rule was less enthusiastic, because the establishment of a Scottish Parliament and the consequent loss of the Scottish Liberal vote at Westminster could be expected to have a fatal effect on the Liberals' tenure of power in England. Though officially Scottish Home Rule was Liberal policy, in the closing years of the nineteenth century and in the years leading up to the First World War, no serious action was taken to implement it.

In the meantime the Scottish Labour Party was founded in 1888. Like the Association for the Vindication of Scottish Rights, it owed an element of romanticism to the support of a literary figure, a traveller, man of letters and upper class radical, R.B. Cunninghame-Graham. But the founder member who stamped his character upon it was James Keir Hardie, a leader of the Scottish Trade Union Movement, who the previous year had become the leader of the Scottish Miners' Federation. The Scottish Labour Party's aims included the nationalization of land, the abolition of the House of Lords, the disestablishment of the Church, and Home Rule for Scotland. Unfortunately for the nationalistic aspect of this programme, the Scottish Labour Party merged with the British Labour Party, and while the other aims of its policy remained among the Party's priorities, that of Scottish Home Rule assumed exactly the same position as it possessed in the Liberal programme: that of an issue to be canvassed when the Party was in opposition, and an issue to be dropped when the Party was in power, in case the Scottish MPs were required to maintain a majority. The force of this was particularly clearly illustrated at the General Election of 1964, when Labour did not win a majority of English seats, but was put into power by the Scottish vote. While the Liberal ascendancy was at its height in Scotland, in the years before the First World War, agitation for Home Rule won another concession when a Scottish Grand Committee of the House of Commons was set up in 1907, to give Scottish MPs the opportunity to deal with Scottish Bills.

The outbreak of the First World War, to a far greater extent than that of the Napoleonic or Crimean Wars, reduced all other issues to insignificance. In a renewed upsurge of British patriotism Scots fought for Great Britain, and for the British Empire, in the creation and administration of which they had played so outstanding a part. But the heroic idealism with which the First World War was entered, the increasing bitterness with which it was fought, and the disillusionment which followed it were also experiences shared by the whole of Britain. The 1920s and '30s were years in which disillusionment, underlined by economic depression, led some Scots to criticize the Union the more harshly, since it seemed that Scotland suffered the after-effects more severely than England.

The First World War had given Scotland's heavy industries a temporarily exaggerated prosperity as a result of the extraordinary demands created by wartime conditions. Coalmining, iron and steel manufacture and shipbuilding had all been called upon to increase production far beyond the limits of peacetime requirements. With the return of peace, not only were the demands of emergency production removed but it transpired that pre-war foreign markets had been lost. With the spread of industrialization throughout Europe, America, and ultimately Asia, countries which had been customers became competitors. The same conditions applied to agriculture and fishing. Scottish farmers, who had increased production to meet home demand during the war, found that in peacetime they had to compete with imported food-stuffs, which were cheaply produced, and could be marketed as freshly as home grown produce, as a result of developments in refrigeration. After the war, the European market for cured herring, once a profitable Scottish export, had been lost; and mysteriously, the great shoals of herring, once so plentiful around Scottish coasts, had themselves disappeared, so that even the chances of supplying a home market had ceased to exist.

Men who returned from the war found that the populist slogans for which they had fought 'A War to end War' and to make 'A Land fit for Heroes to Live in' had been at best fatuous optimism, and at worst wartime propaganda. The depression, which began to be felt in 1921, hit Scotland particularly hard, since its industry was so narrowly based. At the height of the depression, in 1931, there was 65 per cent unemployment in the shipyards of the Clyde, and once again the critics of the Union blamed the sufferings of Scotland on mismanagement by Westminster.

Economic hardship and the failure of any major political party to take serious account of Scottish demands for a greater say in government led to the foundation of the National Party of Scotland, in 1928. This was a left-wing organization with a policy of total separation from England. Its aims proved too radical for the Scottish electorate, and its poor showing at the General Elections of 1929 and 1931 resulted in the foundation of the more moderate Scottish National Party, in 1934. The revival of overt nationalism in the inter-war period once again won some concessions from the Government. In 1928 the Scottish Secretary was appointed a Secretary of State, with Cabinet rank, and in 1939 his headquarters was moved to Edinburgh, and established in the newly built St Andrew's House, which contained the departments of Home Affairs, Health, Agriculture, and Education. This administrative devolution was regarded by nationalist opinion as inadequately concessionary, since the economic weakness of Scotland seemed to render it more vulnerable to assimilation with England than ever before. To those who lived through it, the inter-war period seemed to be a time of frustration and hopelessness; in retrospect it does not appear to have had such a negative character. Some aspects of Scottish life showed encouraging vigour.

The Scottish churches gave other Christian bodies an example in reconciliation by repairing the wounds created by the Secessions of the eighteenth century and by the mid-nineteenth-century Disruption. Two sections of seceders had already combined by 1820, to form the United Secession Church, which later absorbed the Relief Church, to become the United Presbyterian Church. The seceders who remained outside this union described themselves as the United Original Secession Church. In 1863, the Free Church absorbed the majority of the United Original Secession and, in 1876, the majority of another body known as the Reformed Presbyterians. By the end of the nineteenth century, there were three Presbyterian churches: the Established Church or seceded, the United Presbyterians, and the Free Church, and three small minority groups which had refused to become amalgamated with any of them. Amalgamation of the larger churches continued with the union of the majority of the United Presbyterians and the Free

Church in 1900. The resultant United Free Church possessed 1700 ministers as against the 1400 ministers of the Church of Scotland. However, the divisive issue of patronage had ceased to exist in 1874. In 1921 the British Parliament abdicated the last of its authority over the Church of Scotland, by conceding it the 'right and power, subject to no civil authority, to legislate and adjudicate fully, in all matters of doctrine, worship, government and discipline'. With the removal of the greatest of all divisive issues of the past, the United Free Church and the Church of Scotland united in 1929.

The great majority of Scottish Presbyterians now belong to one Church. Scottish religious life outside the Church of Scotland at the present time comprises the Presbyterian splinter groups which refused amalgamation, the Episcopal Church of Scotland, and the Roman Catholic Church, which is represented by the small community of 'old' Catholics which survived the Reformation, principally in the Western Highlands and the Isles, and the much larger community of Catholics, mostly of Irish origin, centred upon Glasgow, and reinforced in the twentieth century by Polish and Italian immigrants. There are also small numbers of Methodists, Quakers and other Christian sects, as well as communities belonging to non-Christian religions, which have come into being as a result of recent immigration.

Between the wars a new Scottish Literary Revival took place, of which the leading spirit was Christopher Murray Grieve, born at Langholm in Dumfriesshire in 1892, who wrote under the pseudonym of Hugh McDiarmid. When McDiarmid began to write Scots verse in the 1920s he found that the language which

Burns had revived did not possess the range, flexibility or vocabulary to express his ideas. The previous literary revival had run out of impetus, and most of the Scots verse written in the late nineteenth and early twentieth centuries was merely an enfeebled echo of that earlier inspiration. MaDiarmid had no use for Burns-and-water Scots, and even less use for the forms which national 'bardolatry' of Burns had taken, for Burns's Night dinners, sentimentalization of the man himself, and half-remembered quotation of his works:

> No' wan in fifty kens a wurd Burns wrote
> But misapplied is a'body's property,
> And gin there was his like alive the day,
> They'd be the last a kennin' hand to gie...

> Mair nonsense has been uttered in his name
> Than ony's barrin' liberty and Christ.
> If this keeps spreadin' as the drink declines
> Syne turns to tea, wae's me for the *Zeitgeist*!

These lines are from *A Drunk Man Looks at the Thistle* (1926), a long poem in the form of the soliloquy of a philosophical drunkard, who lies where he has fallen as he wanders home, gazes at a thistle growing beside him, and meditates on the condition of Scotland, humanity, and the universe. With a well stocked mind and an intoxicated imagination his mood alternates sharply between the satirical and the sublime. To write such a poem McDiarmid needed to recreate a literary Scots which possessed the range and eloquence of the renaissance 'makars' and find a vocabulary to express the very different subject-matter of the twentieth century. To do so he used a synthesis of the Scots speech of his native Dumfriesshire, the different Scots vocabulary of other regions, and some of the lost resources of the language, which he discovered in Jamieson's *Etymological Dictionary of the Scottish Language* (1808), and sought to restore to currency.

McDiarmid's passionate concern for Scotland is a constantly recurring theme in his poetry, expressed in poems of widely differing styles:

> Lourd* on my heart as winter lies
> The state that Scotland's in the day,
> Spring to the north has aye come slow
> But noo dour winter's like to stay
> > For guid,†
> > And no' for guid!**

In contrast to this elegiac voice, he used a bitterly satirical tone to castigate old arguments in favour of the Union in *The Parrot Cry*:

> Tell me the auld, auld story
> O' hoo the Union brocht
> Puir Scotland into being
> As a country worth a thocht.
> England, frae whom a' blessings flow
> What could we dae withoot ye?
> Then dinna threep†† it doon oor throats
> As gin*** we e'er could doot ye!

*heavy
†for good, in the sense of 'for ever'
**i.e., not for the best
††thrust
***if

> My feelings lang in gratitude
> Hae been sae sairly harrowed
> That dod! I think its time
> The claith was owre the parrot!

McDiarmid has been credited with reinstating Scots as a serious literary language. The measure of his success is the number of poets who have found it an acceptable medium for serious poetry on all subjects, not only for specifically Scottish themes. Their work can be sampled in *The Scottish Literary Revival* (1968), edited by George Bruce.

What McDiarmid achieved for Scots, Sorley Maclean, born in 1911, achieved for Gaelic, adapting the ancient language to twentieth-century themes, and inspiring a younger generation of poets to write in Gaelic. On the evidence of the dwindling number of Gaelic speakers earlier in the century, the language appeared to be dying. But its revival as a language in which poetry of high quality is being written probably helped to arrest the numerical decline. In 1971 there were 88,000 people bilingual in Gaelic and English, 13,000 of them in Glasgow, and this number represented an increase of one tenth over the previous decade. It is extremely unlikely that all of them read Gaelic poetry, but those who do can have the satisfaction of enjoying a living literature.

Despite the revival of both Scots and Gaelic as languages of poetry, English remained the dominant language of everyday use in Scotland, as the language used in education, in almost all prose-writing, and by the mass media. Some of the poets of the Literary Revival who wrote in Scots or Gaelic also wrote in English, and some used English exclusively. Edwin

Muir, one of the most distinguished Scottish poets of the twentieth century, wrote in English, even on Scottish themes; and the contemporary Orcadian poet, George Mackay Brown, uses English to express an inspiration firmly rooted in Orcadian experience.

The 'linguistic nationalists', as the poets of the Scottish Literary Revival have been called (with some justice, since they contributed a new flowering to their national literature), continued to write during and after the Second World War, establishing a continuing tradition which a post-war generation of poets has developed. During the war, political nationalists were inactive, observing a wartime truce while British patriotism was united in the struggle against Nazi Germany and its allies. Nationalist activity was resumed towards the end of the war, when it resulted in the election of Dr Robert McIntyre as MP for Motherwell, in a by-election in 1945. He lost his seat again a few weeks later, in the General Election which brought Clement Attlee and the Labour Party to power. Attlee himself had given qualified support to Scottish aspirations to self-government, and the Labour victory raised considerable hopes. Labour's Scottish Office issued a manifesto giving high priority to the establishment of 'a Scottish Parliament for Scottish Affairs', and twenty-four of the thirty-seven Labour MPs returned for Scottish constituencies promised to promote it.

In 1947 a 'Scottish National Assembly' was founded, comprising representatives of local government, trade unions, and presbyteries, together with MPs and peers. It voted for the introduction of a Scottish sub-parliament, as an interim measure, preparatory to the establishment of a Scottish Parliament with wider powers. The Labour Government disappointed these hopes, by merely enlarging the powers of the existing Grand Committee of Scottish MPs, in 1948. In October of the following year the Scottish National Assembly prepared a 'Scottish Covenant' (the name of which was obviously intended to echo the 'National Covenant' of 1638), to be offered for signature to the whole of the Scottish electorate. The signatories were to pledge 'in all loyalty to the Crown, and within the framework of the United Kingdom, to do everything in our power to secure for Scotland a Parliament with adequate legislative authority in Scottish affairs'. By 1950 approximately 2,000,000 Scots, out of an electorate of 3,600,000, had signed the Scottish Covenant.

The lack of Government response to this orderly and organized democratic action was widely disillusioning, and resulted in some dramatic gestures of protest. In 1950 a group of young nationalists removed from Westminster Abbey the Coronation Stone (which, even if it had never been the Sacred Stone of the Scots, had gained immense symbolic power through its centuries of hallowed use in England). They took it to the Abbey of Arbroath, where the Declaration of 1320 had been signed. Grudging admiration for this gesture was felt even by Scots of non-nationalist views, and the return of the Stone to London in the boot of a police car was felt to be a tactless and tasteless conclusion to the incident; though it is hard to envisage how the Government could have arranged for the return of the Stone without investing the incident with dangerous political significance.

The Queen's accession in 1952 was the occasion for nationalist resentment that she did not style herself 'Elizabeth I of Scotland and II of England'. A number of new postboxes bearing the royal monogram EIIR were blown up in protest. With the intention of satisfying Scottish sentiment, after her coronation in 1953 the Queen visited Edinburgh to receive the Honours of Scotland (the Crown, Sceptre and Sword of State) in the High Kirk of St Giles. The occasion was not an unalloyed success, for many Scots thought that the Queen should have worn the Crown, instead of merely receiving it, and felt that she had been wrongly advised to wear informal afternoon dress rather than royal robes. The contrast between the Queen's informality and the ermine-caped mantles of the three peers who carried the regalia gave an unrehearsed impression which detracted from the intended pageantry.

Though Scottish sentiment was obviously alive, it was not manifested as nationalism at the polls until 1967, when a Scottish National Party candidate, Mrs Winifred Ewing, won the hitherto safe Labour seat of Hamilton, at a by-election. Mrs Ewing aroused wild enthusiasm by declaring that it was her aim to see Scotland represented at the United Nations between Saudi Arabia and Senegal, and her supporters responded by publicly burning a Union Jack. But this jubilation was short-lived, for like Dr McIntyre before her, she lost her seat at the next General Election. However, at the General Election of 1974 Scottish National Party candidates won eleven seats: the Western Isles, Murray and Nairn, Banff, Aberdeenshire, South Angus, Dundee East, Perth and East Perthshire, Clackmannan and East Stirlingshire, Argyll, Dunbartonshire East and Galloway. With such substantial and well-distributed gains it began to appear that nationalism was becoming a political force to be taken seriously.

On 1 March 1979 a referendum was held on the desirability of establishing a Scottish Assembly (in effect a sub-parliament with 142 members, presided over by the Secretary of State, who would exercise 'quasi-Viceregal powers' and remain a member of the Cabinet). The result of the referendum is best explained with reference to the new regions of Scotland which had been set up in accordance with the Local Government (Scotland) Act of 1972. The regions were: Orkney and Shetland, Highland, Grampian, Tayside, Central, Strathclyde, Fife, Lothian and Borders.

On referendum day 63.63 per cent of the electorate voted, an affirmative vote being returned by Strathclyde, Central, Fife, Highland and Lothian. Orkney and Shetland, Tayside, Grampian and Borders returned a hostile vote. Five out of nine of the regions had voted in favour of the establishment of an Assembly, yet the decision represented only approximately 31 per cent of the voters, whereas the Government had required a 40 per cent assenting vote as a condition of constitutional change.

At the General Election of 1979 the deflation of nationalist optimism resulted in nine of the Scottish National Party MPs losing their seats. The two who remain are Gordon Wilson for Dundee East and Donald Stewart for the Western Isles.

While it is difficult to generalize about any nation, it seems the S _____ ___ the most part, strongly aware of their nationality, proud of their country, _____ about its future, concerned that it should not lose its separate identity and become assimilated with England, as a result of economic and cultural pressures which appear to be more and more hard to resist. These are some of the ingredients of Scottish sentiment; but the step from national sentiment to nationalism is one which the majority of Scots seem hesitant to take. Constitutional devolution is a question which presents many problems, not the least of which is arrival at general agreement on the form that it should take. The problem is endlessly discussed, but many Scots are more concerned with a preliminary question: after more than two hundred and fifty years of Union with England, would Scotland be economically capable of 'going it alone'?

Between the wars Scotland's economic position in relation to England weakened. New industries, such as car and aircraft manufacture, were not developed in Scotland; the centres of these new industries were south of the Border. The enormous emigration from Scotland which took place during the depression – 400,000 between 1921 and 1931 – was a 'brain drain' as well as an exodus of manual workers in search of better conditions. It was followed by heavy casualties in the Second World War, which left Scotland dangerously deprived of young men of initiative and ambition.

In the post-war period many of the trends of the inter-war years continued unchecked. So far as Scotland's heavy industries were concerned, this was in some ways irreversible. As early as the First World War, some natural resources had been worked to the limit. Native iron ore had been exhausted, and iron and steel manufacture were coming to rely upon imported raw materials. The Lanarkshire coalfields had mostly been worked to the point at which they could no longer be run economically. Over the next decades, the demand for coal declined, as oil became the new fuel for ships, locomotives and power stations. But the age of North Sea oil had not yet arrived, and Scottish industry suffered in the hiatus.

Initiative passed to English concerns, and thence to larger international corporations, leaving Scottish industries in many instances in the condition of peripheral (and therefore expendable) subsidiaries. Most of the capital invested in Scottish industries came from England or America: of the £84,000,000 invested in new Scottish firms between 1945 and 1970, £66,000,000 came from abroad, mostly from the United States, and £17,000,000 from England. Similarly, the ownership and directorship of many Scottish enterprises came to be based in England or America, dangerously reducing the opportunities for personal initiative open to ambitious young Scotsmen if they remained in their own country. While England seemed to be prospering at Scotland's expense, there seemed little grounds to expect otherwise than that the most threatening possibility of the Union would be realized: Scotland would be subordinated and sacrificed to English interests, and ultimately assimilated on the most unfavourable terms.

During the last decade there have been signs of a quiet but decisive change of emphasis. The entry of Britain into the Common Market in 1973 meant that Britain as a whole became a subordinate member of a larger union, and began to experience the mixed blessings of a union not entirely dissimilar to that which Scotland had known since 1707. England is in the painful throes of discovering that adaptation to larger interests involves chastening sacrifices in terms of pride, and will probably lead to similar erosions of supposedly sacrosanct national institutions to those which Scotland experienced as a result of the Union.

The analogy is imperfect, as the power of Brussels is far less in relation to Britain than that of Westminster became in relation to Scotland in 1707; but the psychological effect of the weakening of the original 'predominant partner' cannot fail to change the relationship of Scotland and England. It seems foreseeable, with the passage of time, that Scotland will increasingly feel the need of a separate voice in the affairs of Europe.

Internally, Scotland has changed a great deal during the last decade. One of the most dramatic agents of change has been the development of the North Sea oil industry. It has created thousands of jobs in the areas affected, with resultant shifts in the density of population. Between 1971 and 1981 there has been a 54 per cent population increase in Shetland, 35 per cent in Ross and Cromarty, and 26 per cent in Kincardineshire and Deeside. Not all the newcomers are Scots, and not all become permanent residents; nonetheless, the increases have brought new prosperity to these areas, and seem likely to continue to do so. There has been a lessening of population pressure in the original industrial belt of Scotland, which at one time threatened to unite Edinburgh and Glasgow in a single 'megalopolis'. But during the decade 1971–81 Glasgow lost 250,000 people (22 per cent of its population), while Edinburgh lost 8 per cent. Some of these people have moved to other parts of Scotland, not only in the wake of the oil industry, but also to new centres of urban development, like Cumbernauld New Town; others have contributed to the figure of 170,000 emigration over the decade. Of these, some have sought work in other parts of Britain, and others in America, Canada and Australia. The population at the last census in 1981 was 5,117,146, approximately 9 per cent of the total population of the United Kingdom. Despite the small population it is still surprising to learn that only 5 per cent of Scotland is urban. Though the greater cities have lost in population, and the distribution of population over other parts of the country is more satisfactorily balanced, there still remain vast areas of Scotland which are very sparsely populated indeed. This remains true of the more remote parts of the Highlands, which present a changing, but nonetheless apparently insoluble economic problem.

During the second half of the nineteenth century great tracts of the Highlands were converted into sporting estates. In some instances, descendants of clan chiefs sold their inherited properties to English or foreign businessmen to whom a Highland estate was a status symbol, or a source of entertainment for guests who enjoyed deer-stalking, grouse-shooting or salmon-fishing; and the maintenance of these estates required the services only of a very small resident population. In 1882 a failure of the potato crop and its attendant miseries caused widespread antagonism against new landlords, which was not unjustified, even if it was fostered by a less justified romantic view of the past, in which the relationships of chiefs and clansmen were imagined to have been far more mutually satisfactory than they had ever been. Land raids by impoverished crofters led to the establishment of a Crofters' Commission in 1883, the findings of which brought about the passing of the Crofters' Holdings Act of 1886, which considerably eased the crofters' situation by granting them security of tenure, fixing rents, permitting the enlargement of holdings, and allowing the bequest or assignment of crofts. But security still did not make smaller crofts economically viable, and one unforeseen result of the Act was to create a new class of absentee crofters, who abandoned cultivation altogether, and rented their crofts to temporary incomers, in search of the peace and quiet of Highland remoteness, while they themselves sought employment elsewhere.

This is but one aspect of a change in the Highland economy which has been increasing since the nineteenth century: the growth of tourism. Though public transport in the Highlands and to the Islands has deteriorated in recent years, as a result of the closure of the railways and steamer routes established in the nineteenth century, tourism has continued to increase, overloading the congested roads and ferries. Tourism, however, has brought some much-needed prosperity to the Highlands, assisted by the Highlands and Islands Development Board, established in 1965. This organization has also attempted to encourage agriculture and fisheries and small-scale industrial projects, and in general to assist prosperity in such ways as will least disrupt the patterns of local life. However, the problem of the Highlands is not solved, for the imbalance between a small indigenous population and an overwhelmingly large influx of tourists desirous to observe a way of life which is simultaneously envied and threatened, does not seem to offer a satisfactory solution.

It is impossible to write of the period in which the past merges with the present without leaving many unanswered questions. In Scotland, as in all other countries, its inhabitants ask themselves what will happen next, and wonder how much power they have to control their own destinies. It seems clear that such control could only be achieved by constitutional change, in fact by the return of a far more substantial number of nationalist MPs to Westminster than has as yet been seen there. 'The other thing that could produce Home Rule,' as the Scottish historian Professor Gordon Donaldson wrote as long ago as 1974, 'would be for one of the two main parties to adopt it as part of its programme – and, for a change, keep its word.'

Sovereigns of Scotland from Duncan I to The Union of 1707 (with Regnal Dates)

DUNCAN I
(1034-40)

MALCOLM III 'Ceann Mor'
(1057-93)

DONALD 'Ban'
(1093-7)

DUNCAN II
(1094)

EDGAR
(1097-1107)

ALEXANDER I
(1107-24)

DAVID I
(1124-53)

Earl David

WILLIAM I 'The Lion'
(1165-1214)

MALCOM IV 'The Maiden'
(1153-65)

Margaret

Isabel

ALEXANDER II
(1214-49)

Dervorguilla

Robert Bruce
of Annandale

ALEXANDER III
(1249-86)

JOHN BALLIOL
(1291-96)

Robert Bruce
Earl of Carrick

MARGARET 'The Maid of Norway'
(1286-90)

ROBERT I
(1306-29)

Margery

DAVID II
(1329-71)

ROBERT II
(1371-90)

ROBERT III
(1390-1406)

JAMES I
(1406-37)

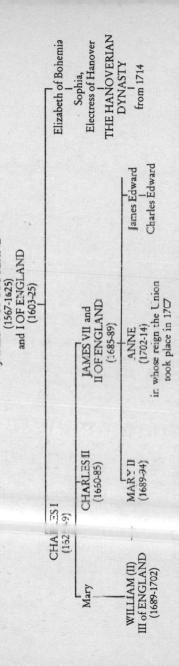

JAMES II
(1437-60)

JAMES III
(1460-88)

JAMES IV
(1483-1513)

JAMES V
(1513-42)

MARY, QUEEN OF SCOTS
(1547-67)

JAMES VI OF SCOTLAND
(1567-1625)
and I OF ENGLAND
(1603-25)

Elizabeth of Bohemia

Sophia,
Electress of Hanover

THE HANOVERIAN
DYNASTY
from 1714

CHARLES I
(1625-49)

Mary

CHARLES II
(1650-85)

JAMES VII and
II OF ENGLAND
(1685-89)

WILLIAM (II)
III of ENGLAND
(1689-1702)

MARY II
(1689-94)

ANNE
(1702-14)
in whose reign the Union
took place in 1707

James Edward

Charles Edward

Books for Further Reading

Ashley, Maurice, *James II* (James VII and II) (1977)

Balfour Melville, E.W.M., *James I, King of Scots* (1936)

Barrow, G.W.S., *Robert Bruce and the Community of the Realm of Scotland* (1965)

Barrow, G.W.S., *The Kingdom of the Scots* (1973)

Bingham, Caroline, *James V, King of Scots* (1971)

Bingham, Caroline, *James VI of Scotland* (1979)

Brander, Michael, *The Making of the Highlands* (1980)

Brock, William R., *Scotus Americanus: a Survey of the Sources for Links between Scotland and America in the Eighteenth Century* (1982)

Bruce, George (ed.), *The Scottish Literary Revival* (1968)

Campbell, J. Lorne (ed. and tr.), *Highland Songs of the Forty-Five* (1933)

Chadwick, N., *The Celts* (1970)

Cole, M., *Robert Owen of New Lanark* (1953)

Cowan, E.J., *Montrose, For Covenant and King* (1977)

Cowan, Ian B., *The Enigma of Mary Stuart* (1971)

Cowan, Ian B., *The Scottish Reformation: Church and Society in Sixteenth Century Scotland* (1982)

Cruden, Stewart, *The Scottish Castle* (1960)

Daiches, David, *The Paradox of Scottish Culture: the Eighteenth Century Experience* (1964)

Daiches, David, *Charles Edward Stewart* (1973)

Daiches, David, *Scotland and the Union* (1977)

Dand, C.H., *The Mighty Affair: How Scotland Lost her Parliament* (1972)

Devine, Thomas M., *The Tobacco Lords: a Study of the Tobacco Merchants of Glasgow* (1975)

Dillon, M, and Chadwick, N., *The Celtic Realms* (1967)

Donaldson, Gordon, *Scotland: Church and Nation through Sixteen Centuries* (1960)

Donaldson, Gordon, *The Scottish Reformation* (1960)

Donaldson, Gordon, *Scotland: James V to James VII* (The Edinburgh History of Scotland, Vol. III) (1965)

Donaldson, Gordon, *The Scots Overseas* (1966)

Donaldson, Gordon, *Scottish Kings* (1967)

Donaldson, Gordon, *Scottish Historical Documents* (1970)

Donaldson, Gordon, and Morpeth, Robert S., *Who's Who in Scottish History* (1973)

Donaldson, Gordon, *Mary Queen of Scots* (1974)

Donaldson, Gordon, *Scotland: the Shaping of a Nation* (1974)

Dunbar, J.G., *The Historic Architecture of Scotland* (1966)

Dunbar, J. Telfer, *The History of Highland Dress* (1962)

Duncan, Archibald A.M., *Scotland: the Making of the Kingdom* (The Edinburgh History of Scotland, Vol. I) (1975)

Dunlop, Annie I., *The Life and Times of James Kennedy, Bishop of St Andrews* (1950)

Dwyer, John, Mason, Roger A., and Murdoch, Alexander (eds.), *New Perspectives on the Politics and Culture of Early Modern Scotland* (1982)

Ferguson, William, *Scotland 1689 to the Present* (The Edinburgh History of Scotland, Vol. IV) (1968)

Fergusson, James, *Alexander III, King of Scotland* (1937)

Fraser, Antonia, *Mary, Queen of Scots* (1969)

Furber, H., *Henry Dundas* (1931)

Grant, I.F., *The Social and Economic Development of Scotland before 1603* (1930)

Grassie, James, *Highland Experiment: the Story of the Highlands and Islands Development Board* (1982)

Grieve, Michael, and Scott, Alexander (eds.), *The Hugh McDiarmid Anthology* (1972)

Haldane, A.R.B., *New Ways through the Glens* (1962)

Hamilton, David, *The Healers: a History of Medicine in Scotland* (1981)

Harvie, Christopher, *No Gods and Precious Few Heroes: Scotland 1914–80* (1981)

Henderson, G.D., *Heritage: a Study of the Disruption* (1943)

Henderson, I., *The Picts* (1967)

Hewitt, George R., *Scotland under Morton, 1572–80* (1982)

Hume Brown, P., *George Buchanan: Humanist and Reformer* (1890)

Innes, Sir Thomas, of Learney, *Scots Heraldry* (2nd ed., 1956)

Insh, George P., *Thomas Muir of Huntershill* (1949)

Johnson, Edgar, *Sir Walter Scott* (1970)

Kellas, James G., *Modern Scotland: the Nation since 1870* (1968)

Kermack, W.R., *The Scottish Highlands: a Short History* (1957)

Kermack, W.R., *The Scottish Borders (with Galloway) to 1603* (1967)

Kinghorn, A.M. (ed.), *The Middle Scots Poets* (1970)

Kinsley, James, *Scottish Poetry, a Critical Survey* (1955)

Lee, Maurice, *James Stewart, Earl of Moray* (1953) (USA)

Lee, Maurice, *Maitland of Thirlstane* (1959) (USA)

Lindsay, Maurice, *Robert Burns* (1954)

Linklater, Eric, *The Prince in the Heather* (the escape of Prince Charles Edward Stuart) (1965)

Linklater, Magnus, *Massacre: the Story of Glencoe* (1982)

MacCaig, Norman, and Scott, Alexander (eds.), *Contemporary Scottish Verse, 1959–1969* (1970)

MacCormick, Neil (ed.), *The Scottish Debate: Essays on Scottish Nationalism* (1970)

Macdonald, D.J., *Slaughter under Trust* (the Massacre of Glencoe) (1965)

MacDougall, Norman, *James III: a Political Study* (1982)

Mackenzie, W.M., *The Secret of Flodden* (1931)

Mackie, R.L., *King James IV of Scotland* (1956)

Maclaren, Moray, *Bonny Prince Charlie* (1972)

Maclean, Fitzroy, *A Concise History of Scotland* (1970)

MacQueen, John, and Scott, Tom (eds.), *The Oxford Book of Scottish Verse* (1966)

MacQueen, John and Winifred (eds.), *A Choice of Scottish Verse, 1470–1570* (1972)

Maxwell, Stuart, and Hutchison, Robert, *Scottish Costume, 1550–1850* (1958)

McFarlane, I.D., *Buchanan* (1981)

Menzies, Gordon (ed.), *Who are the Scots?* (1971)

Menzies, Gordon (ed.), *The Scottish Nation* (1972)

Millar, Peggy, *James* (James 'VIII' and 'III') (1971)

Miller, Karl (ed.), *Memoirs of a Modern Scotland* (1970)

Mitchison, Rosalind, *Agricultural Sir John: The Life of Sir John Sinclair of Ulbster, 1754–1835* (1962)

Mitchison, Rosalind, *A History of Scotland* (1970)

Nicholson, Ranald, *Scotland: the Later Middle Ages* (The Edinburgh History of Scotland, Vol. II) (1974)

Notestein, Wallace, *The Scot in History* (1940)

Petrie, C., *The Jacobite Movement* (3rd ed., 1959)

Piggott, S. (ed.), *The Prehistoric Peoples of Scotland* (1962)

Rait, Robert S., and Cameron, Annie I., *King James's Secret: Negotiations between Elizabeth and James VI relating to the Execution of Mary, Queen of Scots* (1927)

Richmond, I.A. (ed.), *Roman and Native in North Britain* (1958)

Ridley, J.G., *John Knox* (1968)

Ritchie, R.L.G., *The Normans in Scotland* (1954)

Scott, Ronald McNair, *Robert the Bruce, King of Scots* (1982)

Scott, Tom (ed.), *Late Medieval Scots Poetry* (1967)

Smith, Alan G.R. (ed.), *The Reign of James VI and I* (1973)

Smith, Sydney Goodsir (ed.), *A Choice of Burns's Poems and Songs* (1966)

Smout, T.C., *A History of the Scottish People, 1560–1830* (1969)

Stevenson, David, *The Scottish Revolution: the Triumph of the Covenanters* (1973)

Stewart, I.H., *The Scottish Coinage* (1955)

Tomasson, Kathleen, *The Jacobite General* (Lord George Murray) (1958)

Wainwright, F.T. (ed.), *The Problem of the Picts* (1955)

Warrack, John, *Domestic Life in Scotland, 1488–1688* (1920)

Willson, D.H., *King James VI and I* (1956)

Young, Douglas, *Scotland* (1971)

Youngson, A.J., *The Making of Classical Edinburgh* (1966)

Youngson, A.J., *After the Forty-Five: the Economic Impact on the Scottish Highlands* (1973)

Index

Index

Index

Index

Index